Finally a book on applic
in the driving seat – no
or our culture! Packed
the way for newbies and challeng
to rethink their sermon preparation. This will be essential
reading for all my trainees.

Denesh Divyanathan
Senior Pastor of The Crossing Church Singapore
President of Project Timothy
Chairman of the Evangelical Theological College of Asia,
Singapore

It is only as a person turns to apply the Bible that we
see whether they really understand what is meant by
'Expository Bible Teaching'. This outstanding book on
listening to God should be read by every man or woman
who wishes to serve others in the ministry of God's Word.
It will both liberate, from the need to become a sociology
guru; and challenge to listen to God with more humility.
Most of all it will equip for deep and relevant Bible
teaching.

William Taylor
Minister, St. Helen's Bishopsgate, London

This book takes our biblical principles and convictions
about teaching God's Word and connects them straight
to practice. Reading this book made me want to be a
better student of the Bible so that I can better serve the
people I teach. Not just for preachers, this book will get
anyone involved in word ministry listening carefully to

God's word and thinking carefully about application. I'll be recommending it to friends in ministry.

Amy Wicks
Women's ministry, London

Carefully nuanced, with sharp insight, this book expounds key principles for applying God's Word to us today. In doing so, it exposes common pitfalls and habits, as the challenge to listen more attentively to scripture is winsomely brought to life. By revitalising this essential purpose of the preacher's task, this book will prove to be a welcome blessing, not only to the preacher, but to those they serve.

Matt Peckham
Assistant minister, Rock Baptist Church, Cambridge, UK

Get Preaching:

Application

Gwilym Davies

PT RESOURCES

CHRISTIAN
FOCUS

Scripture quotations are from *The Holy Bible, English Standard Version*, copyright © 2001 by Crossway Bibles, a publishing ministry of Good News Publishers. Used by permission. All rights reserved. ESV Text Edition: 2011.

Scripture quotations marked 'NIV' are taken from the *HOLY BIBLE, NEW INTERNATIONAL VERSION* ®. NIV®. Copyright ©1973, 1978, 1984 by International Bible Society. Used by permission of Zondervan. All rights reserved.

Copyright © Proclamation Trust

paperback ISBN 978-1-5271-0535-5
epub ISBN 978-1-5271-0591-1
mobi ISBN 978-1-5271-0592-8

10 9 8 7 6 5 4 3 2 1

Published in 2020
by
Christian Focus Publications Ltd.,
Geanies House, Fearn, Ross-shire,
IV20 1TW, Great Britain

with

Proclamation Trust Resources,
Willcox House, 140-148 Borough High Street,
London, SE1 1LB, England, Great Britain.
www.proctrust.org.uk

www.christianfocus.com

Cover design by Tom Barnard

Printed in Malta

CONTENTS

SERIES PREFACE

In 1592, the Puritan William Perkins published a tract on preaching that he called 'The Art of Prophesying'. He recognised that 'the preparation of sermons is an everyday task in the church, but it is still a tremendous responsibility and by no means easy. In fact it is doubtful if there is a more difficult challenge in the theological disciplines than that of homiletics .'

Since its beginnings in the summer of 1981, the Proclamation Trust has been committed to helping preachers in that tremendous – and difficult – responsibility. We believe that the Bible is God's written Word and that, by the work of the Holy Spirit, as it is faithfully preached, God's voice is truly heard. With Perkins, we are confident that through the preaching of the Word 'those who hear are called into the state of grace, and preserved in it'.

This series of short books is designed to help preachers in that 'everyday task'. Experienced practitioners share their wisdom, gained after years of 'toil, struggling with all his energy that he powerfully works within [us]' (Col. 1:28-29).

We hope that these short books will help all of us to progress in our understanding of the task in hand; to set the novice preacher on a course of faithful preaching; to hone the skills of the experienced preacher; to help preaching groups sharpen one another.

However you use this book we hope that it will achieve its twin aims. That you would <u>get</u> preaching (understanding the task at hand), and get <u>preaching</u> (doing more preaching). May God use these books to renew a commitment in all of us to preach the Word (2 Tim. 4:2).

Jon Gemmell & Nigel Styles
Series Editors

Introduction

There is a scene in Luke's gospel that every would-be preacher would do well to ponder. In some ways the scene is unexceptional – or at least, as unexceptional as a display of overwhelming power over the cruelties of evil can be. Luke's description of the expulsion of Legion in Luke 8:26-39 largely follows the parallel in Mark. The man is helplessly held amongst the tombs. The demons are astonished by the person of Jesus. They beg to be driven into the pigs, pigs that they kill as surely as they were killing the man. The herdsmen flee in terror. And then, when the people come to see what has happened, they find the man clothed and in his right mind. So far, with one or two tweaks for style, so similar to Mark. But here Luke adds a highly significant detail: the man who is now clothed and in his right mind, and who will shortly go out proclaiming the deeds of the Lord Jesus, is sitting at Jesus' feet.

Sitting at Jesus' feet. On the one hand, this evokes that most quintessential of all Luke's pictures of discipleship: Mary, choosing the good portion that won't be taken away, sitting at the feet of her Master. Here is discipleship in a nutshell. Discipleship is to sit and be taught by the Christ when others are distracted by their frantic service. On the other hand, this reflects the whole dynamic of Luke's commission. First, we must be taught by the Lord Jesus. We must have our minds opened to understand the Scriptures, our hearts set ablaze with a new understanding. First, we must read Luke. And only then, rightly instructed by the Master, are we sent into the world to speak of what He has done. And so 'he went away, proclaiming throughout the whole city how much Jesus had done for him' (Luke 8:39). First Luke, then Acts.

It is the expository preacher's mandate. Yes, we must preach. By all means, preach. For the glory of God, and the honour of the Name, and the salvation of the lost, preach. But first, we must sit and listen. Only those who have sat at the Lord Jesus' feet and been taught by Him can presume to speak for Him. Only those who have first given Him ear can open their mouths. You simply won't have anything worth saying until you have listened, carefully, to the Scriptures. The genius of expository preaching is that it is preaching that listens.

And so this little book on application will be a book about listening.

This is not the first book on preaching to connect good application with good listening. In *The Contemporary Christian* John Stott pleaded for preachers to engage in *double* listening. If we're to apply well, we must listen carefully to the Word, and then listen carefully to the world. But that is not quite what I mean. There is, of course, a place for paying attention to the people we are seeking to speak to, and this book will have something to say about that. But this isn't really a book about double listening. Partly, that is because the topic is beyond my competence; partly, that is because double listening is not our mandate. It is the first 'listen', the sustained listen to the words of Jesus, that Luke insists upon. Careful contextualisation might well put oil in the lock. It probably does, and we might even think Luke encourages it. But listening to Jesus is the key.

Listening is underrated at the best of times, but especially when it comes to application. We are always in a hurry. We want to *Get Preaching*. We need to have something to say. We want to be relevant. Our congregations want 'life hacks', and we want 'preaching hacks'. We want shortcuts that will generate armour-piercing application, and do it in haste. Is there a film I need to watch? A journal I can subscribe to? A book I can read? A five-step plan for getting under the radar? And how can I get my congregation to buy into my latest program, to give more, to evangelise more, to serve more, to pray more? It is hard to believe that better, more powerful application will come from working harder at the text.

But it is the conviction of this book that the key to good application is good listening, listening to the Bible. I am not aiming to be exhaustive – there are all sorts of other things that it would be good to say on the topic of application. Some of them are very important, and doubtless there are some that I ought to have included. But it all starts with good listening. First, we must listen long enough to discover that the Bible comes to us pre-applied (chapter 1). Then, we must listen hard enough to hear that the Bible comes pre-contextualised (chapter 2). Then, we must listen carefully enough to hear the claims that the Bible makes upon us, and those around us (chapter 3). Partly, we listen to be effective. I am persuaded that the very best path to incisive, penetrating application is the path of sustained reflection on what God is really saying. The more carefully we listen, the more engaging we're likely to be. But mostly, we listen on principle. If God Himself is commanding, exhorting, encouraging or wooing us, we dare not stop listening until we have understood what He wants. We listen, and we listen, and we listen. And only then are we ready to speak (chapter 4).

'And they came to Jesus and found the man from whom the demons had gone, sitting at the feet of Jesus, clothed and in his right mind' (Luke 8:35). Our aim is to Get Preaching. But we'll need to start by listening.

1
LISTENING FOR THE APPLICATION

The secret to good application is good listening. The better we listen to the Bible, the better we'll apply it. But the trouble is that we often think of application as something we do once we have stopped listening. We might think that application comes *after* listening: once you have worked out what the passage is saying, you need to think about what it means for you and your hearers. Or we might think that application comes *before* listening: you begin with an idea of the thing you'd like to achieve, and then you find the passage that you hope will do it. Either way, response is severed from attentive listening. You may listen after you apply. You may listen before you apply. If you're at all interested in expository preaching, you'll certainly want to listen at some point. You listen for the big idea, because the Bible is authoritative over our attempts to construe its meaning. But then the application is not about listening. It is in your hands. Does the Bible have authority to constrain our response? Is application about listening?

The argument of this chapter is that it is. Good application really does come from good listening. But first, it's worth exploring how our approach to application might *stop* us from listening carefully to the Bible.

Application and a listening deficit

Using the Bible

The most obvious way in which application might get in the way of attentive listening is when we want to use the Bible to achieve our agenda. At the extreme end, this is obviously offensive. One of the Cornhill staff once heard a sermon on 'breakthrough' from Mark 2:1-12. We can achieve breakthrough in our lives by imitating the desperation, the determination and the daring of the paralytic's friends. It is difficult to imagine that the preacher spent very long listening to Mark's gospel at all. From the outside, this looks like a sermon that began life as the speaker's desire to speak on 'breakthrough', a suitably trendy theme. The desire then grew legs, arms, eyes, and scoured the gospels for a text until it happened upon a passage where some people broke through something – in this case, a roof. The careful student of Mark might point out that neither the friends nor the man are the primary subject of this episode, however laudable their determination might have been. Far better to focus on Jesus, or even the religious leaders. The careful student of Mark might ask whether Mark himself would have had any notion of the preacher's idea of 'breakthrough'. But the point is that this preacher wasn't interested in studying Mark; he only wanted to use it.

The temptation can come in a much subtler and worthier form. We detect that our congregation is lacking in evangelistic zeal, and so we prescribe them the medicine of Philippians to get them behind gospel partnership. We have an upcoming building project, and so we reach for Nehemiah. We're about to make a statement on sexuality and gender, so we teach our way through the opening chapters of Genesis.

In many ways, this is absolutely right. Peter Adam has helpfully described the Bible as a medicine cabinet, full of different spiritual medicines to treat different spiritual conditions. Part of our job as preachers is to plan sermon series. Far better to ask, 'what does this church most need to hear now?' than 'what would I like to have a crack at next?' If we detect a need for change, we should want the Word of God to lead it.

Nevertheless, the danger remains. Peter Adam's metaphor presupposes that we're good enough pharmacists to understand our medicine, and good enough physicians to understand our patients. We ought to be. But the agenda can take over. Every sermon on Philippians becomes a fresh call to evangelism, whether or not that is Paul's intention. Every sermon on Genesis 2-4 becomes a position paper on sexuality, gender, and work, whether or not that was Moses' aim. The good desire to reach for the right medicine to treat this specific ailment has taken over, and we're no longer really listening. Was Moses trying to achieve something else? Was he medicating a different condition? I'm unlikely to notice.

Spotting applications

There is a second way in which the rush to apply might stop us from listening: we might settle for *spotting* applications. For example, a preacher working through Mark 1:35-39 might make hay with verse 35. Here is a mandate for the Christian quiet time: 'The Lord Jesus himself made a priority of prayer. He made a priority of prayer by withdrawing from society. He made a priority of prayer by rising early. He made a priority of prayer even when his friends did not understand him. And in the same way, we ought to make a priority of prayer too.'

We might think that this is harmless enough. There is nothing wrong with prayer, there is nothing wrong with encouraging it in a sermon, and there's nothing wrong with taking Jesus as an example. But this application did not come from listening to Mark, and Mark has not taught us about the priority of prayer. It came from a pre-existing list of worthy applications, derived from a combination of the imperative sections of New Testament epistles and the preacher's evangelical heritage. The preacher listened to Mark just long enough to notice something that sounded like good Christian application, to *spot* it, and then he was ready for launch.

This is the trouble with character studies in the Old Testament, teaching 1-2 Samuel to learn lessons from David or Judges to learn lessons from Samson. It's not that this is inherently wrong. There is a place for enjoying the heroes of the Old Testament (let's call it Hebrews 11). And often enough, we are supposed to associate with, or dissociate from, the behaviour of the characters in Old Testament narrative. In all sorts of ways, Abraham, David, Jonathan and Joshua *are* exemplary. Even Samson has his moment in the sun.

But the problem comes when character study becomes a reading strategy: the only reason we turn to the text is to learn lessons from the life and conduct of a Bible hero. And the problem with this reading strategy is that it bypasses the intention of the text. We don't wait for the cues that this is the way the author wants us to respond. And we don't locate that response within the bigger picture of the author's message about God and His purposes. We don't ask what response this part of the Bible is itself calling for, or why this book was written. In practice, we come to the text with a pre-existent list of commendable behaviours. And then we read until we spot them, surreptitiously skipping over any unsavoury bits. Our application is likely to be Christian, because our list is basically right. But we haven't been taught by the Bible. And if the Bible author wanted us to imitate his main character here, we're right by fluke and not design.

In either form, this approach ought to bother us. It ought to bother us that application is something we're bringing to the text we're teaching, rather than getting out of it. It ought to bother us that our list of worthy applications becomes almost impossible to reform. What if there is *nowhere* in the Bible where the author himself intends us to draw the application we keep spotting in Old Testament characters? We're unlikely to notice. It ought to bother us for its tendency towards moralism, and there will be more to say on this in due course. But most of all, it ought to bother us because just at the point we turn to response, we stop listening.

Thinking up applications

There is one more approach to application that displays
a listening deficit. This is the most subtle of all: we might
think that it is our job to 'think up' the application. Imagine
a sermon on Isaiah 40:10-26. Having worked hard at
the text, you conclude that this passage is all about God's
incomparable sovereignty. It is the Lord, and not the
nations of the earth or their idols, who rules over heaven
and earth and the fate of nations. He is utterly sovereign.
And so you turn to apply. 'How can I apply the fact that
God is incomparably sovereign? Well, I suppose it means
that I ought not to be angry when the photocopier breaks
down as I'm printing my sermon. And I ought not to be
anxious about the results of the General Election. And I
can turn the other cheek when my colleague wrongs me at
work. And I can avoid taking out the extended warranty
on my computer.' And the list goes on.

On the one hand, this seems right. Surely, if we
genuinely understand the point of the passage, that God
is incomparably sovereign, it will have an impact on
all those areas where we live as though God were not
incomparably sovereign. The list we've just given isn't a
terribly bad start. More than that, the kind of thinking on
display here is closely related to the sort of thinking we
will need to do to apply well (more on this in chapter 3).
At some point, working through the specific implications of
big picture principles will matter.

But then there's the other hand. The problem, again,
is that we have stopped listening too quickly. We have
listened to Isaiah 40 just long enough to extract a

theological proposition from it, and then we've tried to work out what to do with that proposition. Isaiah 40 is there to tell us a truth, but it's our ingenuity that puts that truth to work. We have to work out how to use it. This is inattentive. We haven't noticed that Isaiah was never merely articulating a theological proposition: Isaiah was calling for a response. Before we work out how we might apply the truth of God's incomparable sovereignty, we might begin by asking how *He* does.

The Bible comes pre-applied

The problem with all three of these approaches to applying the Bible is that they stop listening to the Bible too quickly. When we just want to *use* the Bible, we barely listen at all. When we content ourselves with *spotting* applications, we listen badly, waiting to hear what we already knew. When we 'think up' applications, we set out to listen well, but break off much too soon. If we listened just a little longer, we would realise that the Bible comes pre-applied. It is already calling for a response. It is already speaking to achieve a purpose. We simply haven't listened hard enough until we have heard what that purpose is.

One way we might describe this purposefulness is from the perspective of the human authors of Scripture. Every one of the Bible writers wrote pastorally, calling for a response from the people of God. This is transparent in the epistles, where we can clearly see the apostles writing to effect change: the rejection of false teaching, perseverance in the gospel, identity formation or repentance from worldliness. It's also there in the gospels:

Luke writes to give Theophilus certainty (Luke 1:4), John to summon and strengthen faith (John 20:30-31), Mark that we might repent and believe (1:14-15). The whole Hebrew classification of the Old Testament reminds us that these are books that were written to change people: Law, Prophets, and Wisdom – instruction, appeal, and insight. Sometimes this is obvious. It would require a particular sort of tone-deafness to miss the note of appeal that runs through Deuteronomy. Sometimes, it is more subtle. We might forget that the great narrative of Joshua–2 Kings was never just telling us what happened. But it wasn't: this history was written to change people. It was written to rebuke idolatry, to explain calamity, and to give hope in the face of exile. In other words, it was *prophetic* (which is how the Hebrew Bible categorises this history: the former prophets). And so viewed from the perspective of its human authors, Scripture is pastoral theology. Part of listening properly is listening long enough to discern their pastoral intent.

Alternatively, we might prefer to think in terms of the divine author.[1] The Word of God never comes to us as mere information: it is always personal. But because it is personal, it demands response. God Himself is speaking to us. If He speaks to command, we are required to obey (Exod. 19). If He speaks to promise, we are summoned to trust (Gen. 15). God reveals Himself so that we might know Him in covenant (Exod. 3). God speaks so that we might have life (John 5). It would be different if the Bible were just a collection of pious thoughts about God,

---

1   Not that we ought to divide the divine and human authors.

an anthology of Christian mysticisms. Then, perhaps, we might be free to isolate those thoughts and apply them as we deemed fit. But if the Bible is God Himself speaking, and 'men spoke from God as they were carried along by the Holy Spirit' (2 Pet. 1:21), then there is a person behind it.[2] Personal communication requires a response: 'God speaks so that we can understand him and respond appropriately.'[3] God speaks to achieve a purpose.

Whichever way we approach the question, the point is the same: the Bible itself is summoning us to respond.

This isn't really a new insight. Of course, there are ways to make it sound modern and up-to-date. Tim Ward and Kevin Vanhoozer have made excellent use of 'Speech-Act Theory' in their accounts of Scripture and hermeneutics respectively.[4] Our speech is an act: it is designed to achieve things. Or we can think about it anecdotally. I vividly remember being asked three times at a dinner party whether I'd like more pudding. I declined each time. I would have done so indefinitely if it weren't for the kind soul who helped me to understand that the old Etonian I was eating with was asking me to pass *him* the pudding. Words do things – or at least, they're meant to. They are purposeful. The Proclamation Trust has been saying it for

---

2   Three excellent books on the Bible that explore the Bible as God speaking are *God Speaks* by Rich Alldritt and Ash Carter, *Words of Life* by Timothy Ward, and *The Doctrine of the Word of God* by John Frame.

3   John Frame, *The Doctrine of the Word of God* (Phillipsburg, NJ: P&R, 2010), 3.

4   Tim Ward, *Words of Life* (London: IVP, 2009). Kevin J. Vanhoozer, *Is there a meaning in this text?* (Grand Rapids, MI: Zondervan, 1998).

ages. An experienced preacher recently reminisced about a PT preaching group he'd been in. He was asked to give a sermon on 1 Corinthians 10:13. He preached it as a great word of encouragement. Inevitably, Dick Lucas pointed out that he'd turned the passage on its head: 1 Corinthians 10 is a rebuke. To take it as an encouragement is to misconstrue it. It is Speech-Act Theory and common sense and PT orthodoxy.

But the insight is crucial: if we haven't understood what a person's words are trying to *achieve*, we haven't understood them. If we don't know what words are trying to *do*, we haven't listened long enough. I simply hadn't understood my friend when I failed to pass him the pudding. The preacher simply hadn't understood 1 Corinthians 10 when he failed to notice that it was a rebuke. And of course the good news is that it means that the Bible comes pre-applied. Application isn't something that we bring to the Bible, it is something we derive from it. Had the preacher listened a little more carefully, he wouldn't have needed to find an application for an otherwise inert Scriptural truth. He would have found that Paul is already calling for a response. Isaiah is already calling for a response. Mark is already calling for a response. If we listen long enough, the Bible will tell us what it requires of us and our hearers. The Bible comes pre-applied.

And so the secret to good application is careful listening. We need to listen to the Bible long enough to understand its purpose: what was this passage written to achieve? What response is the living God calling us to?

The Bible's 'pre-application' matters

The trouble with listening is that it takes so long. Discerning a serviceable main point from Isaiah 40 might take a few minutes; understanding the purpose of Isaiah 40-55 will take hours, or weeks. Understanding purpose requires context, whole books, back-story. It means exchanging a glance for a stare, a pricked-up ear for a furrowed brow. Why is it worth taking the time?

Firstly, it will make us more *effective*. If we think that the Bible has been written well – whether we are thinking in terms of its human or divine authors – then it will have been written to effect its own purposes. The whole shape of Isaiah's argument in chapter 40 – the details, the rhetoric, the persuasion – all of it will have been crafted to change his readers the way that he wanted to. The truth of God's incomparable sovereignty is already under orders, marshalled to achieve the prophet's purpose. Or the Spirit's purpose, we might say equally. The words will be most effective when they are put to the use for which they were written. And so when we use Isaiah 40 to remind people not to get cross with a malfunctioning photocopier, we're using a scalpel to knock a tent-peg into the ground. It's not that we can't do it, but there are better ways to use a scalpel and there are quicker ways to erect a tent. Partly, it is about effectiveness.

Secondly, it is worth taking all this time to listen because we are under *authority*. To fail to attend to the Bible's own purposes is to be doubly presumptuous. To begin with, it is presumptuous to hear the living God speak and not listen carefully enough to understand His command. The problem with taking Mark 1:35-39 as a mandate for quiet times, or 1 Corinthians 10:13 as an encouragement in temptation, is that we haven't really listened. The living God was speaking. He was addressing us, with words He wanted us to hear, to achieve the purpose He chose. But we didn't think it was worth listening long enough to understand what He required. We listened just long enough to find something that would preach. This is perilously inattentive, especially when we're speaking of the Word of God. It is not at all clear that God cares more about our propositional rightness than our obedience. So why would we formulate an approach to the Bible that makes it authoritative over its truth-claims but not its application?

But more than this, it is presumptuous to take those divine words – words we have not understood – and assign them a purpose of our own. Luke gives us a category for the desire to harness the power of God's words without submitting to their agenda: magic. The confrontation between the gospel and magic is an important theme in Acts. It bookends the third quarter of the book, Acts 13:1-19:20, encircling most of Paul's missionary activity. And it opens the second quarter, as Peter stares down the other Simon in Samaria. In both quarters we see that one of the first things to happen when the gospel invades the Gentile world is the overthrow of magic.[5] Partly, this is about money. Where the apostles eschew silver and gold, magic is big business. Partly, it is about power. It is power that Simon wants to hang on to, and strength

---

5   I remember hearing this in a Dick Lucas sermon on Acts 8.

that the sons of Sceva fail to harness. Significantly, it is about manipulation. For Simon and the sons of Sceva, the proclamation about Jesus is something they can use. It is not a personal word, a word with a Master behind it who commands obedience. It is a magic charm, that can be directed where they will. But they are wrong: the magicians always lose, the Word confounds their schemes, and they are driven out humiliated. The Word of the Lord continues to increase and prevail mightily (Acts 19:20). It is not that the preacher who takes Mark 1:35 as an exhortation to prayer is of a piece with the incantations of the sorcerer. That preacher is marked by a different spirit, the Spirit of submission to the Lord Jesus Christ. But his hermeneutic is not so different. He may not have cast spells, and he won't be driven out naked. But he hasn't really listened either. He just wanted a word he could use. Understanding the purpose matters – even if it is hard – because we are under *authority*.

But finally, it is worth taking the time to listen because we want to apply *rightly*. Downstream of magic, we find moralism. The difficulty is that our agendas are often so much smaller, and so much more 'activist', than the Bible's. The Biblical authors aim for the big beasts of application: faith, hope, love, a renewed mind, a heart of wisdom. We want to pick off a few sparrows: come to church, bring a friend, give to the gospel. The Bible wants us to grasp grace, trust a promise, know the Lord. When we're listening carefully, there's just a chance that we'll hear these messages, and communicate them carefully. But when we take matters into our own hands, we don't. In theory, this is

not absolutely inevitable. It is possible to imagine a world
in which the agendas we bring to the Bible tended away
from activism. We might use a Bible passage to increase
our congregation's view of God, or their grasp of grace.
If we were good enough pharmacists, we would. And
sometimes we do. But more often, when we enlist the Bible
in the service of our plans, we want it to do something
more practical. So the horizon of our application shrinks.
Certainly, we seldom *spot* applications like 'Jesus is utterly
unparalleled' from our pre-existing application lists.
We're too busy telling people about the priority of prayer.

    And so, because it will make us more effective, and
because we are under authority, and because we want to
apply rightly, we need to make sure that we listen.

Learning to listen again

The key is to let the author's purpose constrain our
application. Sometimes the tweak will be obvious. Both
our Markan preachers would have done much better to
remember that Mark is the 'good news of the Son of God'
(Mark 1:1), and better still had they noticed the command
to 'repent and believe the good news' (Mark 1:14-15).
Whatever Mark 1:35 might say to our prayer lives, 1:35-
39 is primarily a word about the priorities of the Lord Jesus.
Not, in this case, the priority He gave to prayer; rather, the
priority He gave to a ministry of proclamation. Mark 2:1-
12 helps us to see why. On the one hand, His ministry of
proclamation is unpopular: it is only after this pivot point
in 1:35-39 that Jesus begins to attract hostility. But on the
other, it is necessary. The good news is not good news that

can be enacted. It is not about the final rollback of evil – at least, not yet. It is about the proclamation of *forgiveness*. This is what the Lord Jesus has come to use His authority to do: to proclaim the forgiveness of sins. Both Mark 1:35 and Mark 2:1-12 are much more about Jesus than about us, much more about grace than our goodness. But they are also much more challenging for it: these episodes open our eyes to what we really need, to what the Lord Jesus came to do, to why the world so readily rejects Him, and to why He stubbornly refuses to fall in step with our agenda all the same. The truth is that Mark just had bigger and better ideas than our preachers credited him with. He got them from Jesus.

Listening for the author's purpose isn't always easy. Thinking really clearly about the purpose of Isaiah 40 would require a book-length study, decisions about the context of Isaiah's hearers and the relation of Isaiah 40 to chapters 1-39. This is hard work. But no one ever said that preaching was meant to be easy; listening is the good portion, but it's not free. And besides, it wouldn't take *really* clear thinking on Isaiah 40 to improve our message from the one we 'thought up'. We would only need to notice that this is a chapter that begins with comfort, that declares good news, and that tells those who have been waiting that God has not forgotten them. We didn't need to read the whole of Isaiah to find out that Isaiah's primary aim isn't to console us about a malfunctioning photocopier. He had bigger fish to fry.

And it can take us by surprise. I was recently involved in a sermon series on the opening chapters of Genesis. We embarked on the series because we had issues we wanted to address – mostly around sexuality and gender. But that wasn't what we found. We started on Genesis because we wanted to shore up our convictions on a particular topic – and we did. But for the most part our sermons were on the bigness of God, the futility of secularism, the sheer grandeur of the human calling and the devastating loss inflicted by sin. Above all, we were confronted by our need for the gracious Word of God to put our sin-torn world back together again. We were aiming for sparrows. The Word of God was felling monsters. We were so glad to have taken the time to listen.

The secret to good application is good listening. And that is true, firstly, because the Bible is already summoning us to respond.

2
LISTENING TO BE SHARP

The secret to good application is good listening. But how do we make our application *sharp*?

We do want our preaching to be sharp. There are ways of being sharp that shouldn't interest us. There's no value in looking clever: for most of us, incisive cultural commentary is a temptation that we probably ought to resist. And there are ways of being sharp that are beyond our power. We only have a limited part to play in the work of spiritual heart surgery: we don't hold the scalpel. Our work will only ever take a person so far. But we do want to be understood. We want the implications of God's Word to be understood. We want our message to be heard. We want it to 'get under the skin' – to get close enough that our encouragements will be heard as real encouragements, our rebukes as real rebukes. So how do we make our preaching *sharp*?

Sharpness is not quite the same thing as specificity. It is tempting to confuse the two: the more our sermons are heard as a specific word, a word of direction for very particular situations, the sharper we think we're being. And so we multiply examples, targets, in our talks: what might this mean for the youth group tomorrow, the single woman this Friday, the retiree at Christmas, or the curate in Tuesday's staff meeting? It's not that specificity is without value, and we'll have a little more to say on this in the next chapter. But if this sort of specificity is the same as sharpness, we need to face the reality that lots of the Bible isn't very sharp at all.[1] Ephesians and Colossians might sketch out the shape of the Christian life, but they hardly drill down to the habits of Mrs Jones in the supermarket on Thursday mornings. And they're at the extreme end of the spectrum. The fact is that the Bible is not, for the most part, very specific in its application. And yet it is sharp. Hebrews must have felt like a slap in the face to the congregation that first read it. I bet it got right under their skins. It just didn't give them all that much to do.

So sharpness is not really about specificity. It is more about proximity. Or, to use a slightly more dangerous word, relevance. To be sharp is to preach a message that feels close to home – a rebuke that feels like it understands us, understands us well enough to be a true rebuke. It is to give an encouragement that feels like it gets us, an encouragement that gets us enough to actually encourage us. In other words, it is not blunt. It does not bounce off and leave us unaffected. It is not a message that leads us to spectate from a distance, to observe, give a score, and then move on. It is relevant not because it is up-to-date

---

1   There is another kind of 'specificity' that is certainly characteristic of the Bible: its message is addressed to specific people at a specific point in time, rather than to humanity as a generality. We will have much more to say about this in due course. But for all the specificity of its audience, its message is normally couched in pretty general terms.

and trendy, but only in this: it is clear that it really does address us.

We want our preaching to be sharp because we really do want to get through to people. So how do we do it? How do we make our application *sharp*?

Listening to today's world to be sharp?

Our first assumption is often that the best path to sharpness is to spend more time listening to the culture around us, what John Stott termed 'today's world'. On the face of things, this makes a tremendous amount of sense. Surely, the more we listen to people, the better we will understand them. The better we understand them, the more able we will be to make our message feel close. If we really listen to people, we will be better equipped to encourage those in need of encouragement, to exhort those in need of exhortation. If we really listen to the culture, we will be better able to address it: its hopes, dreams, flaws, and concerns. And of course, if we want to be more specific, we will certainly need to spend more time listening to people: we can hardly apply to Mr Thomas' Wednesday afternoon unless we know something about what he actually does with his life. And so, in the pursuit of sharpness, we listen to the world. Because we want to be sharp, we download podcasts, we subscribe to *The Economist*, we watch the news and tune in to the occasional radio debate. If we're feeling especially erudite, we read the Man Booker shortlist or buy anything that makes it into Tim Keller's footnotes. And then we try to think about how our message applies to each of those who will hear it, we work our way through the specifics of their lives. We assume that the shortest path to sharpness is to spend more time listening to today's world, or to those we're seeking to address, or both.

There's a sense in which this is obviously right. Translators know that they need to listen to their target language. There would have been no sense in trying to translate the Bible into English if someone hadn't taken the trouble to listen to the English speak. More than that, translators need to know something of a culture. At the time of writing, the activist Greta Thunberg is backpeddling, with some desperation, from her call for world leaders to be put up against a wall. Apparently, she assures us, that all sounds very different in Swedish. And so preachers need to know how to break out of their own bubble, and be understood by people living in what sometimes feels like another world. I have heard more than one sermon that really was delivered in a sort of Christianese. To the Christians in the room – or at least, those who had grown up in that particular church tradition – it was all very helpful. Or at least somewhat helpful. But it was so carefully wrapped up in Christian vocabulary, sentiment and cultural expression that there was next to no chance that an uninitiated hearer would be able to discern the real content. The speaker sounded impervious to the real world; as he was to the world, so was the world to him. He spoke in English, but it might as well have been another language. We learn new languages by taking the time to listen to them. And so if we want to be able to make ourselves understood, we certainly will need to listen to the world. And we will need to keep on listening to check that we really are getting our message across.

But that isn't quite the same thing as saying that listening to the world is what makes us *sharp*. Sharpness isn't just about being understood. It is about showing that you understand – that you really understand your hearers, that you really are addressing them. In other words, sharpness is not just about clarity of expression, about finding the right words to get your meaning across. It is about proximity, about relevance, about saying the thing that these people need to hear. Certainly there are those who think that listening to the world is the right way to get *sharp*. But this little book about application is really a book about listening, and my suggestion is that the very best way to be sharp is to listen more carefully to the Word.

Listening to the *Word* to understand the *world*

If we want to be sharp, we need to listen to the Bible more carefully. The best way to be relevant is to sit a little longer at Jesus' feet. And this is true in the first place because it is the Bible that tells us who we really are.

The Bible is able to tell us about ourselves because, it insists, there is a basic homogeneity to human culture. To begin with, there is the Bible's insistence on analysing human cultures theologically. For example, Isaiah describes Assyria as 'Babel' in his thirteenth and fourteenth chapters. This is not mostly because Assyria claimed the Babylonian crown (although as a matter of fact she did). Rather, it was because Isaiah wanted his hearers to understand that the very best starting point for understanding Assyria was the ancient account of the Tower of Babel in Genesis. And there is a second reason he calls her Babel. He also wants his hearers to understand that she is fundamentally of a piece with the Babylonian Empire to come (Isa. 47). Two superpowers, separated by decades, but both explained by a text plucked from the very beginning of Genesis. In the same sort of way, John calls Imperial Rome a beast because he wants his readers to understand that this empire is cut from the same cloth, with the same lawless, anti-Davidic, dehumanising tendencies as Daniel's monsters. He calls the city Babel, and Sodom, and uses Isaiah's oracles against Tyre and Sidon against her. Babylon, Rome, Sodom, Tyre, Sidon: here are cultures separated by centuries, by languages, and by thousands of miles. And yet they are essentially the same. If you want to understand Rome, just look at Babel. Or better, go back to the very beginning and look at the serpent. The Bible's theological descriptions of human culture teach a basic homogeneity between what might appear to us to be radically different societies.

But this basic homogeneity is even more obvious when we notice the way that the Bible extends it even to Israel. In Romans, for example, Paul is at pains to include Israel in his account of Adam. Having begun with a description of Gentile Pagans that evokes the third chapter of Genesis (Rom. 1:18-32), Paul turns to the people of God. And he insists that they are every bit as much 'man' as everybody else (Rom. 2:1, 3; 3:5; 9:20). Of course they share in Adam's guilt, part of the 'all flesh' that cannot be justified by the Law (Rom. 3:19-20). But they also share in Adam's culture: they suppress the truth, they make excuses, they answer back to God, they defend the lie. Even as they seek to deny their similarity to the Pagans, they only underline their Adamic suppression of the truth. John makes the same point in different terms. Every one of his references to 'the world' could easily be substituted for 'unbelieving Israel'. It would be a mistake to make the substitution: he really is talking about the world. But that is precisely the point: Israel is just like the rest of the world. Unbelieving Israel *is* the world. They are every bit as much the heirs of Genesis 3 as the most darkened Pagans. Here is the deepest cultural divide in all the world – Israel versus the Gentiles. But at the deepest level, they are just the same.

Firstly, then, the Bible *can* help us to understand ourselves because there is a fundamental unity that stretches across all human cultures. But more than that, we *need* the Bible to help us understand ourselves because we're such unreliable interpreters. Nowhere is this more obvious than in John chapter 8. The Jews who believe in Jesus think that they know themselves: they have always been free, they are right, they are the family of Abraham, they are children of God. They also think that they know Jesus: He is controlled by a demon, a Samaritan, a blasphemer. But the truth is that they are liars – and they prove themselves to be liars as they call Jesus a demon-possessed Samaritan. And they are murderers – and they prove themselves to be murderers as they pick up stones to kill Him. And most strikingly of all, they are slaves. As Hebrews this ought to have been their badge of honour: they are a nation of freed slaves. Instead, they reject it categorically: 'we have never been enslaved to anyone' (8:33). But this denial is not only historically and theologically illiterate, it is also palpably untrue. At every turn, and without the slightest trace of self-awareness, they prove their slavery to sin as they follow their Satanic father in his murderous and deceitful opposition to the Son. But this ought to sober us. If they had been asked to give an account of their culture, they would have missed all its most salient features. Jesus is the only truth-teller in this chapter. We need the Word of God to show us what we're like because we're so bad at understanding ourselves.

And this is why the Bible is quite happy to tell us what we're like. Acts 17 is often given as the parade example of contextualisation. Here is Paul, addressing the Athenians in their own terms, repackaging what has thus far been an essentially Jewish message for the Gentiles. He has listened carefully to the Athenians, we might think, he has understood their culture, and this has equipped him to articulate his gospel in Gentile-friendly terms. But this is a serious misrepresentation of what is happening in Acts 17. For the most part, Paul's speech in the Areopagus is not about the gospel; it is about Athenian culture. And far from repackaging the gospel to make it more relevant to the Gentiles, he is redescribing their own culture from a hostile biblical perspective. Preposterous though it might seem, the apostle is *telling* them about what they are like. Mostly, they are ignorant (17:23, 29, 30). And his source material is not so much a careful analysis of Athens (which he may or may not have had time to conduct); it is his knowledge of the Hebrew Scriptures. It's not that Paul has listened to the culture so that he might better explain the Bible; he's listened to the Bible to explain the culture.

And so the first reason why sharpness comes from listening to the Word is because we need the Bible to tell us what we're like. We do not know the truth about ourselves, but the Bible brings light into the darkness. And there is enough continuity between Babel and Birmingham, Rome and Rio, Sidon and Sidmouth, that we can expect the Bible to describe us accurately. The point is not that we will never listen to the world. Of course we will – we will only be able to understand the language we need to speak as we listen to its native speakers. And we will need to know our society well enough to spot our beasts, our prostitutes, our Tyres, and our Babels. But it's not that we listen to the world to understand our culture, and then work out which bits of the gospel resonate most deeply. No, we listen to the Bible to understand our world, and then we look at the world to see how the Bible's anthropology is currently cashing out. If we really want to be *sharp*, we should start by listening.

Listening to a Word that is already *sharp*

But there is a second reason why it is listening to the Bible that will make our application sharp: this is that the Bible is *already* sharp. The Bible was written to get under people's skins. The Bible comes to us pre-contextualised.

What do I mean when I say that the Bible comes to us pre-contextualised? We have already seen that the Bible is not a list of theological propositions waiting to be repackaged into a message. It is a message: it speaks with purpose, and it comes pre-applied. But neither is the Bible a generalised message, vaguely addressing everyone, precisely addressing none. Each of the books of the Bible speaks into a context. They address specific people, with specific temptations, a shared history and particular pastoral needs. In this sense, each Bible book is already *sharp*.[2] When the Corinthians opened their mail in 55 AD, they didn't need to work out how to read 2 Corinthians in such a way that it would get under their skin. They didn't have to turn its undifferentiated message into a rebuke for them, an appeal to them. Paul had already done that. He was already addressing them.

We're used to thinking of this as a problem – precisely the problem, in fact, that contextualisation is required to fix. Because the Old Testament was originally written in Hebrew, and the New Testament in Greek, they need to be translated. Because Isaiah originally addressed the people of Jerusalem in the seventh-century BC, we need to think hard about how he addresses us as Christians. Because Paul wrote to the Corinthians, he didn't write directly to us. Much that is difficult about understanding the Bible is the natural consequence of the fact that it was written into particular contexts. We don't imagine that Moses, or Isaiah, or Paul meant to be opaque. Insofar as we find them opaque, it is because we are reading someone else's mail, hearing an encouragement or a rebuke directed to people in another age and place. And so we might be tempted to regret the way the Bible

2   It is in this sense that the Bible is 'specific'.

was written. We might wish that it had been packaged differently, as a series of general messages directed to the whole of humanity. Fifty executive summaries, perhaps, in the fifty primary languages of human civilisation.

But this is a mistake. There's no denying the fact that the particularity of the books in our Bibles gives us work to do. But this is part of the glory of God's revelation. This is a point of theological principle: we must assume that the eternally wise God did not make a mistake in the way in which He chose to reveal Himself. If there were no revelatory value in our receiving epistles directed to churches far removed from us in place and time, these epistles would not be in the Bible. The fact that they are in the Bible implies that there is some benefit to us in hearing this sort of divine revelation.

And that benefit is precisely that we get to hear a message that is already *sharp*. We're not left to wonder how the theological generalisations of the Bible might interact with the realities of life. We see it in action. We see it because we hear the message of Kings as a message delivered to this people (Israel), with this theological backdrop (the Pentateuch), at this point in time (the crisis of the exile). We see it because we hear the message of Colossians as an appeal to these Christians (Gentiles in Colossae), facing these temptations (Col. 2:16-23), at this moment in Paul's missionary career (his imprisonment). In other words, we can turn the 'problem' on its head: Isaiah preached to real people in the seventh-century BC, and we get to listen in! Paul wrote to real Christians in first-century Corinth, and we get to hear what he said!

The balance of this is quite wonderful. In the Old Testament we witness the growth of a nation under God, tracing their story from the calling of Abraham to the exile and beyond. We see their Scriptures aggregate as an interpretive backdrop. We watch their story unfold. And so at every point, we are able to hear Scripture as they would have heard it, as a timely word directed to these participants in this grand history. And then in the New Testament, we see what it means for us to be invited in. We see the climax of Israel's history in the gospels. But then we see the questions that that climax throws up addressed in *these* epistles to *these* specific churches at *this* point in time. At every stage, the message of the Bible is historically specific. And precisely because it is specific, it is also *sharp*.

The point of all this is that it gives us a path to sharper application – the path of careful listening. If we want to understand how the words of the Bible really bite, then we need to begin by listening more carefully. How would they have bitten for their first hearers? How would they have heard the rebuke? Where's the encouragement for them, in their circumstances? It is the old preaching instruction: 'Go to Corinth!' It is the triangle tool: God speaks *to* them then, *for* us now. But sharpness needs to come from the whole triangle. It's not that the arrow to 'them then' gives us an undifferentiated message, and then the arrow to 'us now' makes it sharp. It's not that we listen to the Word for the truth, and then to the world for a target. On the contrary, all the sharpness of our journey to 'us now' will come from our grasp of the sharpness of God's Word to 'them then'. The better we hear how this was relevant to them, the better we'll discern its relevance to us. The closer we approach and empathise with the author's intended reader, the nearer his words will feel. And so listening carefully to the Word puts arrows in the quiver *and* shows us where to aim. The path to sharp application is good listening.

There are ways of getting this wrong. It is not that we seek to reconstruct the original hearers from extra-biblical information – archaeology, or extra-biblical literature, or scholarly attempts to reconstruct the traditions behind the text. Neither is it that we use the text to hypothesise a Christian community at radical odds with the rest of the early church (a favourite pursuit of New Testament critics) – a community that invented the text to meet their needs. And neither is it that we weave elaborate reconstructions based on decreasingly probabilistic readings of minor details. It is possible that the man who caused pain in 2 Corinthians 2 is the same man who had his father's wife in 1 Corinthians 5, but it'd be foolish to rest too much weight on it. It is possible that the Ephesians were grieved by Trophimus' implication – however blameless – in Paul's arrest. But I would be nervous about making this the interpretive crux of the epistle he sent them. No, if our 'them then' are not relatively clear from the text, we should be very cautious about fabricating a 'them then' that the text does not give us access to. We need to make sure that we really are *listening*, and not inventing a tune of our own.

We don't need to invent a tune of our own, because each of the Bible books really was given to a 'them then' that we have been given some access to. The Bible comes pre-contextualised – and whatever difficulty this adds to the task of exegesis, it also adds considerable sharpness to its message. Every book of the Bible really was addressing real people, with their real failures and concerns.

This is the second reason why good listening is the path to sharp application. We ought to listen to the Word because the Bible draws near to deliver its message to people in all their particularity. The more closely we see how this really did engage *them*, the better we'll grasp what it means for *us*.

Getting sharper in practice: Revelation and Malachi

The path to sharpness in application is the path of careful listening. On the one hand, this is because we need the Bible to tell us what we're really like. God's Word is the best cultural analyst that we have. On the other hand, the Bible comes pre-contextualised – it is a sharp and relevant Word, and we'll hear its relevance to us as we take the trouble to hear its relevance to those who first heard it. This double case for careful listening might sound like it's coming from two very different poles: we are seeking to uphold an essential *homogeneity* that unites us with people living in the seventh-century BC with one hand, whilst arguing for the importance of a *particular* message to a specific people at a specific moment in time with the other. In reality, though, the two come together. We only really understand the Bible's theological anthropology as we see it applied at a moment in time.

Revelation

Certainly, this is the case with Revelation. Revelation is a book that is not shy about telling us what the world is like. Revelation is a cultural analysis, and as we've already seen, it describes culture in theological and therefore general terms. But we often miss the force of this for failure to think hard enough about the 'them then'. One of the mistakes we make in reading Revelation is to assume that the reason that it paints the world in such lurid colours is that this was what life felt like for its first readers. Revelation, we imagine, is a book for the persecuted church, fighting for survival in the face of the totalitarian state. It is painted with a fluorescent palette because at a time like this the ordinary colours won't do.

And yet this is to get things entirely back to front. If we take the time to listen to the seven letters to the seven churches, we see that overt persecution was a relatively distant threat for most of them. Smyrna was facing some sort of civil persecution; Philadelphia was enduring the slander of their Jewish neighbours; Pergamum can look back on the martyrdom of Antipas. But Antipas is history at the time of writing, and Philadelphia and Smyrna are exceptional: the other four churches seem relatively comfortable. They are under enough pressure to encourage compromise, but nothing out of the ordinary.

This is profoundly significant. It means that Revelation is an *unmasking*. John does not describe Rome as a prostitute, the emperor as a beast, and life as a war because that is what life felt like for his readers. On the contrary, he wants them to know that in spite of their comfort, they are in a war. Despite its attractions, Rome is a vicious prostitute. Behind his 'peace', Caesar is a monster, a merciless tool of the dragon. And this has implications for us. We also live in a war that feels like peacetime, in a city that seems attractive, under a rule that seems beneficent. And we also need to realise that behind the masks there lies a prostitute that would seduce us, a monster that would destroy us, a war that would overwhelm us and a dragon that would devour us. Insofar as we live in a society that also contests the Lord Jesus' exclusive claim on the world's worship, we need to be willing to repaint our world in the same lurid colours.

The whole purpose of Revelation is to draw back the veil so that we can see what is really going on with the world. But we will only see the significance of this as we listen carefully enough to realise that for the original readers as for us, this is not the way the world appears. Revelation is the Word of God telling us what our world is like – but we will only feel the force of this as we draw near enough to the 'them then' to hear John's message in all its original sharpness.

Malachi
Malachi treads a similar line: it is a word of diagnosis, telling us about ourselves. But it only bites as we draw near enough to empathise with its first readers.

It isn't hard to hear the word of diagnosis on *them*. The people are self-deceived. They think that God has not loved them, they can't see how they are despising His name, and they don't understand why He is not accepting their sacrifices. They think that God is failing to bring justice to them, and that it is therefore pointless to serve Him. But in the face of their self-righteousness and their self-deception, Malachi tells them what they are really like. The priesthood are despising His name and corrupting their covenant. The people are faithless to the one God, wearying Him, even robbing Him. They are a nation of covenant breakers, and they are in very great danger: when the Lord God does act in the day of His power, there is every chance that they will be set ablaze. Looking in from the outside, it isn't hard to see this as a word of judgment on them.

But it is hard to empathise. It does not feel very close to home. Surely, we might think, we are not like them.

This is why it is worth digging a little deeper into the 'them then': how is it that they could be simultaneously so half-hearted, so transparently faithless, and yet so self-deceived and self-righteous? The answer comes from putting Malachi into its biblical context. Malachi speaks after the exile to those who had returned to Jerusalem from Persia. For one thing, this ought to remind us that these are the remnant. Malachi is not preaching to recalcitrant backsliders who couldn't be bothered to act on God's promises. He is preaching to those who had taken risks. His audience are the faithful ones, those who had uprooted their lives in exile, in Babylon, to make the dangerous journey home to an impoverished city with little to commend it. They are the remnant. But more than this, it ought to remind us that they had expectations. The reason that that return had felt worthwhile is because they had Deuteronomy 30 etched into their minds. After the exile, there would be a double return: the people would return to the Lord (had they not done that?), and He would return them home to abundant peace and blessing.

But this explains their half-heartedness. It is not the half-heartedness of those who have never really bothered. It is the half-heartedness of those who have made decisions for God, who have taken big risks, and have been disappointed. It is the half-heartedness of those who think that being one of God's people doesn't really make a difference. But importantly, it is the half-heartedness of those who think that they have arrived at that conclusion through experimentation. They gave God a go, and He let them down. This, in fact, is simply what they say: 'It is vain to serve God. What is the profit of our keeping his charge or of walking as in mourning before the LORD of hosts?' (Mal. 3:14). Why did we bother? They tried going all out for God. Or at least, their parents did. And it didn't change a thing. And so whilst they are going to retain the shape of their religion (they're not ready to throw it over yet), they will reduce the cost. They will still offer expensive sacrifices, but they will find a way to make them a little less expensive. The priests will still teach the people, but not when it gets them into trouble. They will still live in the land, but they'll make the prudent marriage arrangements they need to. They will stay Christian, but without any of the vim.

And suddenly, it is all much closer to home: we can well imagine how we might end up thinking very much like this. And so the Word of God to them – your disappointed half-heartedness is actually covenant-corrupting, name-defiling, one-God denying faithlessness – is suddenly very sharp. There's still some contextualising to do. We aren't under the same covenant, we aren't waiting for the new Elijah, the Temple and priesthood have been fulfilled. And so the shape of our response will be different. We'll still need to navigate the trip from 'them then' to 'us now', and do so with care. But that won't be what makes our arrow sharp – it is plenty sharp enough already. And it is sharp for the same double-reason that we saw in Revelation. Malachi cuts through our self-deception to tell us what we're really like, diagnosing conditions that we didn't know we had, painting in a scheme we didn't know we needed to use. And it is able to cut through *our* self-deception as we listen carefully enough to know the 'them then', and to realise that in all the most important ways, they are too much like us.

Conclusion

And so if we want to be sharp, we will need to listen. If we want to be relevant, we will need to listen. Better application and better preaching does not come from rushing to the pulpit. Nor does it come from rushing to YouTube and our army of cultural analysts. The more carefully we listen to the Word of God, the better we will understand our world, our hearers, and ourselves. The Word of God understands us in our generality: it gives a theological anthropology that we can apply to every age and culture. But it also understands us in our particularity: because this Word was delivered to a particular people, at a particular point in time, we're given a people to draw alongside, a mirror to hold up to ourselves, a window on where the Word of God really bites. And so if we want our preaching to be sharp, if we want to be relevant, to understand the people we're seeking to win, if we want our words to get through to them, we need to be better listeners. The longer we sit at Jesus' feet, the sharper our sermons will become.

3
LISTENING TO LAND THE APPLICATION

How do you land the application?

To this point, this has been a book about listening. I've argued that listening is the key to getting application right. We need to listen to the Bible long enough to realise that it comes pre-applied: God is already speaking with a purpose, to summon obedience, faith, repentance, and love. We need to listen to the Bible long enough to realise that it is already sharp. The Bible understands us, it tells us about ourselves. The Bible comes pre-contextualised - and as much as this can make it harder to understand, it also opens it up. The Bible is a near word, delivered to real people in the midst of their real lives. This book has been a manifesto for listening, and for avoiding the false start of breaking off from our listening too quickly.

But at some point, we will want to make the journey from 'them then' to 'us now'. We have listened long enough to discern why God is speaking. We have listened long enough to hear that this is a near word, that really does resonate with what we're like. But what does it mean for us? At some point, we will need to 'land' the application.

At this point, we might think, it is appropriate to stop listening to God's Word, and to start speaking, or listening to the world, or thinking about it. Perhaps we might draw up a representative list of people that we can work through to try to land the application: Yuli, to represent the young mums; Richard, for the newly retired; Tracy, for the parents of difficult teenagers; Warren, for the formerly keen-bean now worn down by work; Simon, for the long-term singles; Greta, for the bright-eyed graduates with their future before them. Or we take our laptop to the coffee shop to help us connect our thinking with the real world. Or we go back to *The Economist,* or the radio, or our parish visiting, or our copy of Charles Taylor. We've avoided all the false starts, we've listened carefully, and now it's time to get our heads out of the Bible and to listen to the world. Or at the very least, to think about it.

And this is almost true. Certainly, there's nothing wrong with any of the approaches outlined in the previous paragraph: I have a copy of Charles Taylor, I sometimes run through this sort of a list, I occasionally watch the news, and I've probably been spotted finishing a sermon in a coffee shop. But even here, there is a danger that we might break off from listening to the Bible too soon. This, after all, is a book about listening. And the argument of this chapter is that even as we seek to *land* our application, we will want to retain that same basic stance. As we bring the application across to 'us now', we must still be those who are listening carefully to God's Word, sitting at Jesus' feet.

The principled case for landing the application through listening

Partly, this is a matter of high principle, for the very simple reason that the very first person we ought to 'land' our application of the Bible on should be ourselves. This is true whether we think of ourselves as disciples, exegetes, or preachers. And as disciples, exegetes and preachers, it is dangerous to stop listening too soon.

First, then, we must hear the application to ourselves because we are *disciples*. This ought to go without saying, but sometimes it needs to be said. Christian preachers do not work for the divine postal service, and we are not passing on someone else's mail. If the purpose of a passage is to exhort, it is an exhortation to us. If it is to encourage, it is an encouragement to us. God spoke to them then for us now, but the 'us' includes 'me'. The Word that I preach to others stands over me. The living God is addressing me. And this is the primary reason that we must sit at Jesus' feet before we speak for Him. It is not simply that we need to be trained by Jesus before we work for Him. Neither is it that we need to be drilled – to make sure that we have got the message completely straight so that we don't lose it in transmission. It is that we are disciples, who need God's Word of correction, command, comfort and commission for ourselves. As disciples, it would be wicked to have heard the Word of God and given no thought to its claim upon us.

Secondly, though, we must hear the application to ourselves because we want to be good *exegetes*. This might feel like a step backward in the argument – haven't we moved on from exegesis to the task of application? But things are not that simple. In the Bible, understanding and obedience are intimately linked. This point is made powerfully in Isaiah 28. Ever since Isaiah 7, the Lord has revealed His purposes – and they are repeated again here. The proud crown of the drunkards of Ephraim will be overthrown, and the Lord of hosts will be a crown of glory to His people. Assyria will invade, she will overflow the banks, but she will be stopped at the gates of Jerusalem. The priests and the prophets reject this word as childish riddles, a nursery rhyme foreign policy: 'To whom will he teach knowledge, and to whom will he explain the message? Those who are weaned from the milk, those taken from the breast? For it is precept upon precept, ... line upon line, here a little, there a little' (Isa. 28:9-10). In the midst of a time of foreign policy upheaval and international disruption, God's Word seems like an irrelevance. But the result of their rejection of the Word as childish riddles is that this is what it becomes to them: The Lord said, '"This is rest, give rest to the weary; this is repose," yet they would not hear. And the word of the LORD will be to them precept upon precept, line upon line...' By the end of the chapter, the Lord is still promising the same salvation through judgment, but now it really is in riddles: 'Give ear, and hear my voice; give attention, and hear my speech. Does he who ploughs for sowing plough continually? Does he continually open and harrow his ground?' (28:23-24).

The point is sobering, and it is repeated one way or another in each of the four gospels. A failure to listen to God's Word leads to foolishness. If we toss the Word of God that we do understand to one side, the Word of God will come to us in riddles that we can no longer penetrate. Unbelief leads to blindness. And whilst it is possible to be surprisingly effective as a blind servant (Isa. 42-45), this will be no good to *us*, and this is not *Christian* ministry. And so if we want to be able to understand God's Word for others, we need to make sure that we hear it for ourselves.

Thirdly, we see the same truth when we think about what it means to be a *preacher*. We should be careful about collapsing Old Testament prophecy into the work of giving sermons. In the first place, we risk claiming too much for ourselves: there are ways in which I am not Isaiah, Jeremiah or Ezekiel. And then secondly, we risk taking too much away from our brothers and sisters: Luke insists that insofar as we have the name of Christ on our lips, every Christian is a Malachi, an Elijah, an Ezekiel and a Jonah.[1] But there is significant truth to the parallel between Old Testament prophets and New Testament preachers: Timothy is the man of God, after all. And so, insofar as the parallel stands, one thing ought to strike us: the internalisation of the Word of God is foundational to the prophetic vocation. Ezekiel must eat God's Word (Ezek. 2:8-10). Jeremiah embodies His message.[2] Isaiah, like Moses, must walk the path of the people he serves ahead of them.[3] The work of preaching begins with personal encounter. To be a preacher, we must swallow the message.

From all three angles, the point is clear: as a matter of principle, we must not leap to apply to others before

---

1   C.f. *Get Preaching the Cross* (Fearn, Ross-shire: Christian Focus, 2019).

2   Andrew G. Shead, *A Mouth Full of Fire* (London: IVP, 2012).

3   Isaiah 6. See John N. Oswalt, *The Holy One of Israel* (Eugene, OR: Cascade Books, 2014).

we have taken the time to respond ourselves. To do so is dangerous – dangerous to our discipleship, to our understanding, and to our vocation. And so whether or not it makes us more effective, we should make sure that we have heard, that we have really listened. If we jump from 'them then' to 'you now' without first stopping at 'me', then we've jumped too far, we've missed our first mark, and who knows where gravity will take us. We land the application on 'us' first as a matter of principle.

The pragmatic case for landing the application through listening

But there is also a pragmatic case for taking the time to listen well for ourselves before we rush to think of others: it will make our application better. The primary reason for this is that it will help us to avoid the danger of applying to a straw man, a stereotype.

The trouble with stereotypes is that they are alienating. It's not that they have no purpose. I spent several years in Singapore, and to prepare me for my arrival the Singaporean pastor of my church gave me a briefing on Singaporean culture. He tried to explain the ways in which Singaporeans are different from their British counterparts – different attitudes to money, possessions, authority, career, family, and education. And as a thumbnail sketch, it was genuinely useful. It helped me to orient myself, to begin to adjust my expectations. But it was quickly apparent that I couldn't make a habit of preaching to the stereotypical Singaporean without alienating half the room. Partly, that was because plenty of Singaporeans don't fit the stereotype — they simply didn't recognise themselves in the caricature. Partly, it was because even those who did, to some measure, didn't really like being told what Singaporeans are like by a slightly superior ex-pat. (It might be worth pointing out that this is not just a danger for those working in cross-cultural settings. I wonder whether students and bankers always appreciate being told what they're like from the pulpit.) But mostly, it's because the stereotype was always a cardboard cut-out, a two-dimensional man. It wasn't really *anyone*. And so as I applied to the stereotype, it was always going to distance people: 'but that isn't really *me,* even if he thinks it is'.

Straw men creep in so easily. And so many of our favourite strategies for landing the application positively encourage them. When we ask, for example, how a passage might apply to the youth group, or to young mums, or to retirees, or to city workers, we're practically inviting the straw men to come into our studies and pull up a chair. When we lean too heavily on amateur cultural analysis, we're lending them a rug and a pair of slippers. We end up giving evangelistic talks as though everyone has been reading *The Guardian:* we preach to the intelligentsia in their absence. At Cornhill we occasionally hear practice talks introduced with one or two made-up characters — ideal types with an invented name, the kind of person to whom the speaker thinks this message most readily applies. The fiction is always transparent: I'm never taken in. This kind of ideal type is just a straw man with an alliterating name. And the result is that a device that was intended to help land the application – or at least introduce it – just pushes it further away.

The only real defence against this invasion of straw men is to find some real men and women to apply to instead. And of the three most obvious ways to find a real, flesh-and-bones, three-dimensional target for landing our application, at least two of them involve the preacher listening more carefully to the text.

The first real person: 'them then'

The first place we might find some real, flesh-and-blood human beings to apply the Bible to is in the work we've already done on the 'them then'. This is why attending carefully to the 'them then' helps us to get sharper. It doesn't leave the message of the text as an abstraction, a message simultaneously summoning all and none. But more than that, it also helps us to avoid the risk of only applying our message to made-up people. Even if all our thinking about our audience is entirely stereotyped, without the slightest trace of texture or nuance, a genuinely empathetic understanding of the impact of Malachi's message on his first hearers will mean that we've included at least *some* more or less three-dimensional people in our attempt to land the message of the sermon. For this reason, it can actually be quite helpful to spell out the implications of a passage for its first hearers in our sermons: it gives our hearers a first run at hearing this message applied to some real people, even if they're never really convinced we understand *them*.

The second real person: the preacher

But the second 'real man' that the preacher can apply the message of the passage to is *himself*. We've already seen that we ought to do this on principle: as disciples, as exegetes, as preachers, it is essential that we pay attention to what we hear. But the other advantage of listening carefully for ourselves, really mulling over the implications for us, is this: to the extent that we know ourselves, we've found another real person upon whom to land our message. When I think hard about how the Bible ought to change me, I'm no longer thinking in clichés. And because I'm a real person, and my image of the young mum is not, listening carefully to the application for myself will do more to help the young mum than just about anything else I can do.[4]

At first glance, this might seem surprising. Surely, we might think, the working woman or the recently retired salesman is too different from the middle-aged Christian minister for his personal reflection to be of much use to them. But for at least three reasons, this is mistaken. First, it forgets that the most important application is not about the little things that we do. It is about the big beasts of faith, hope, and love – instruction, encouragement, and exhortation. This is not to deny that people are different: of course we are, and those differences matter. But we are *most* different at the level of the specifics of what we'll be *doing* on Monday morning. At the big picture level, we

---

4   Of course, that's not to say that it isn't *also* a good idea to then think about distinct groups within a congregation. Or even to talk to them. We'll get to this in due course.

are more similar: the dynamics of living by faith aren't so very different for any of us. Secondly, it neglects the point we started with: a well-intentioned application to a straw man (or woman) is much more alienating than a genuine application to a real, but very different, human being. The truth is that the average Singaporean student may well be more similar to me than they are to my stereotype of a Singaporean student. The woman on the thirteenth row who is barely able to work because of ill health may be more like me than my stereotype of someone in her position. Genuine application to me has the not inconsiderable advantage of being genuine. But thirdly, it misses the fact that it doesn't really matter that we're different anyway. Even if the way the truth lands for me really is *very* different from the way it lands for someone else, I can still exemplify the *kind* of thinking they'll need to do to bring it across to them.

And so precisely because I want to have something to say to people who are not like me, I'll want to make sure that I really do listen carefully for myself. I'll want to draw as close as I can to the 'them then' – how am I like Revelation's first readers? How might I be tempted to forget that I'm in a war, that there is an enemy prowling, that compromise and complacency are deadly? Where do I feel the pull of economic pressure or political power? Where might I be tempted to be complicit in the great project to rob the Lamb of His praise? How have I forgotten that Jesus is on the highest throne, that the throne is drawing near, and that His eyes are all the while upon me? But then having thought about how I am like the 'them then', I'll want to think about what their message means for me. How does this change the way I view the world? How does this change what I think the present time is for? How does this change my view of God? The Lord Jesus? The world? My calling? How might I need to repent, or to keep enduring? In other words, I'll want to meditate, and to pray. And perhaps, just occasionally, to present some of the challenge to me from the pulpit. Because an authentic word on my response is likely to be more genuinely three-dimensional than my attempts to describe the right response for others.

The second 'real man' I can apply the message of the passage to is myself. And so again, the longer I listen to the Bible, really listen, the better I'll apply.

The third real person: someone else

I've suggested that there are two ways to land the application on a real person that are really about listening to the Word: I think through what this would have meant for them then, and I think through what it means for me now. But there is a third way to land the application that doesn't involve me thinking up applications for other people from the comfort of my study: I could talk to someone. I could ask a friend what they think it might mean for them.

For most of our Cornhill students, this is a truly revolutionary thought. I was recently chairing a preaching practice group where we had two perfectly good evangelistic talks on John, but where neither talk had anything much to say to a Christian. For this reason, they were badly underdeveloped: they each had an evangelistic appeal, but there was no real hint that this might challenge, or encourage, or change any of us. I pointed this out to one of the preachers, and they said 'I know, but I just hit a roadblock. I couldn't think how this might make a difference to a Christian.' I might have pointed out that he had broken off listening too soon – if he'd really thought hard about John's purpose for his *original readers*, he would have had something to say to Christians. If he'd thought harder about how it might encourage or challenge *him*, he'd have something to say to Christians. Instead, I suggested that he might have asked a Christian friend: how do you think this passage might encourage us?

I do this all the time. When I'm trying to prepare a sermon I ask my wife, Jenny, my colleagues (thank you, Stephen and George!), my students. Once or twice, I've even tried sounding out my six-year-old son. Mostly, I ask my wife. I vividly remember a week a few years ago that I was speaking on Colossians 2:8-15. I felt every bit as stuck as the Cornhill students I've just mentioned. I thought I knew what this meant for 'them then' – don't be tempted by the synagogue: everything it could possibly offer you, you already have in Christ. But I didn't feel even vaguely tempted by the synagogue, and I was sure that none of the people I was going to speak to did either. How might we feel a lack, a deficiency like the Colossians? What would that look like for us? And so I thought, and I prayed, and I thought, and I spoke to Jenny. And somewhere in that chatting, something began to get clearer: what made the alternatives appealing in Colossae was that their

Christianity was so 'bare'. They had no historic buildings, no publishing houses, no parachurch organisations and no Christian record labels. They didn't have a band on a Sunday, or a pulpit, or an established liturgical tradition. They didn't even have a complete New Testament; they probably didn't have a complete Old Testament! 'All' they had was the fact that they had heard a message from Epaphras, and believed it. And perhaps they had a tattered copy of Isaiah that one of them was able to read. *That* was why they felt that the synagogue might be able to offer more. And when we saw that, we began to see that the gospel very often feels 'bare' to us. We want to dress it up as much as they did – whether in traditions, or experiences. We might not hanker for the Temple, but we might very well try to recreate it. My wife and I weren't tempted by the synagogue. But as we talked, we found that we were often dissatisfied with the 'bare' gospel. I often find that my Christian friends ask questions or share insights that sharpen my understanding of a passage. And even more often I find that they have helpful things to say about how the purpose this passage lands.

The important thing to notice is that even here, we haven't really moved on from listening to the Word. There are ways that we could have done this. I could just spend time with people in my congregation to find out what they're like, to hear their struggles and their hopes and their failures. This would be genuinely beneficial, and I'm quite sure that it would help my sermons. And even if it didn't, it would give me plenty of opportunity for ministry – opening the Word with them there, equipping them to preach the Word in all of life. But that's not quite what I've been describing. No, I've been describing a sort of 'corporate listening'. You think you've understood the purpose of a passage. You've begun to work out where it might land for us. And then you ask some brothers and sisters to think that through with you, to listen humbly together, to wrestle with what God is saying to us. You're still listening to the Word, but you're in company. You've asked a friend to sit in the armchair to keep the straw man outside just a little longer.

Landing the application on us now

There's a danger that the argument of this chapter might be misunderstood. It might be heard as a very critical word on all sorts of helpful practices. That is not my intention. Taking the time to remind yourself of your congregation – the different people at their different stages in life – is bound to be helpful. Remembering to mention the different theatres of life – work, and home, and study, and recreation, and friendship, and church, and neighbourhood – may help people to connect this message to the life they actually lead. And there's a place for thinking about how your message would apply to representative people. (Although it's always better to pick a real individual rather than a category. We're generally much better at describing the struggles and questions of people we know than we are at inventing hypothetical representatives.) Building relationships, working with people, engaging in personal work – these are good steps towards landing application well. Watching the news probably isn't a bad idea, and I quite enjoy listening to audiobooks that tell me something about the culture. My aim is not to outlaw any of these things, or even to discourage them.

But the danger is that we think that these things are the key to deep, penetrating, incisive application. The danger is that we stop listening much too fast. We don't really get clear on the purpose. We don't really get clear on what it meant for its first readers. We don't really get clear on what it means for us. And then we expect to generate something powerful and incisive and deep through our knowledge of society and our engagement with philosophers.

We are expository preachers, and so we need to slow down. The only things we will ever have to say that are really worth saying are the things that we have heard from God. And so, we must listen. Even as we seek to land our application, we must listen. The path from 'them then' to 'us now' is still the path of listening. Because the key to good application is good listening.

4
LISTENING TO SPEAK

What will we actually say?

The main thrust of this book has been that we need to guard ourselves against trying to speak too soon. The first task of the preacher is not to speak. Our first task is to listen. And so from at least three different perspectives this book has been an encouragement to slow down, to listen a little longer, to make sure that we really have heard the Word of God. We will apply better if we don't break off from listening too soon.

But eventually, we will want to speak. We do not remain chained to our desks indefinitely. We must not be the sort of students who can never bear to face the vocation they've been trained for. Most of us don't have the option: Sunday is always coming. And so the aim of this series, that we *Get Preaching*, is absolutely right. Neither the liberated demoniac nor Mary sat at Jesus' feet forever. In the end, it is time to go on our way proclaiming. Luke comes first, and then Acts. But the time for Acts does come.

So what will we actually say? How does all the work we've done on careful listening cash out in our sermons? And does it make a difference to their structure, their shape, their overall thrust?

The argument of this final chapter is that it should. Precisely because the application is not an add-on to the meaning of the text – because *all* the work we've done on application is rooted in careful listening, our application ought to dictate the shape of our sermons. In fact, we can put this more strongly: to the extent that our application is genuinely the product of careful listening, we're actually undermining our *exposition* when the structure of our sermons makes application sound like an afterthought.

And so this final chapter is about how we turn all our careful listening into the outline of a talk. Because it's procedural, this chapter will inevitably feel a bit more bitty than the three chapters that precede it. But I hope it will also help to put flesh on the bones: what difference might really careful listening make to the kinds of things that we say?

Application as an afterthought

Before we turn to how we might do things differently, it's worth examining why it is that we might need to consider change. The truth is that it is more than possible for application to be an afterthought in our preaching. And some of our most cherished wisdom on how to put together an expository sermon doesn't help.

Here is an outline of a not untypical Cornhill preaching practice talk. The preacher is speaking on Romans 4. He has a decent enough theme sentence: *Paul's gospel of justification by faith for all is consistent with the Old Testament.* He has a decent aim sentence: *Greater confidence that the gospel of justification by faith for all is in line with the Old Testament.* And his outline looks like this:

Introduction	Illustration from politics about how undermining it is when people change their minds, to introduce the question of whether God has changed His mind.
Point 1	**Justification has always been for free** (4:1-8)
Illustration 1	I remember how good it felt to get my first pay cheque. It was so good to have something that I'd earned. But we need to understand that justification has never been like that.
Application 1	We need to stop thinking that the things we do earn righteousness before God, e.g. quiet times, giving, gospel ministry.
Point 2	**Justification has always been for all** (4:9-16)
Illustration 2	Timing matters. Imagine a songwriter accused of nicking someone else's song. It'd make a massive difference if you found the dated file that showed they actually wrote the song *first*. And timing matters with Abraham. Because he was justified *before* he was circumcised, justification can be for all.

Application 2	We need to realise that the gospel is not just for our type of people. Whoever our neighbours are, whatever background they're from, we ought to reach out to them.
Point 3	**Justification has always been by faith in God's power to raise the dead** (4:17-25)
Illustration 3	Willingness to believe a word depends on the character of the person speaking. Jury service.
Application 3	We can trust that God will keep His promises – even when they seem impossible.
Conclusion	Because justification has always been this way, we can be confident in proclaiming the gospel.

This is an invented outline. But it is not particularly unrepresentative, and I don't think it's a straw man. In fact, it isn't a very bad effort at an expository outline. Personally, I don't think the theme or the aim quite get to the bottom of what's really going on in Romans 4, and I think the idea that justification 'has always been' this way needs a bit more thought. But Romans 4 is a tricky chapter. One or two of the illustrations are a little bit tired, and the aim sentence could be expressed more elegantly. But I don't think many past or present Cornhill students would be particularly ashamed of this talk. Truth be told, it is pretty standard fare.

And yet it is difficult to avoid the impression that the application is indeed an afterthought here. This is in spite of the fact that the student has worked hard to apply his sermon. At three different moments in the talk, he has paused to draw out the implications for us. An outline like this gives no indication of whether the preacher developed their application at length, or brushed past it. But for the sake of charity, let's imagine that each of these three 'applicatory moments' were carefully drawn out. He has worked hard on application. But for all that, the application has all the hallmarks of an afterthought.

The first problem is that each of the preacher's three points is applied in an essentially different direction. Is this talk calling us to repent of legalism, or to evangelise unlikely people, or to trust God's promises even when they look unlikely? The answer is 'all of the above, in more or less equal measure'. But this means that at least at the level of its application, the sermon is fundamentally divided (the pleasing syntactical symmetry of the points notwithstanding). T. David Gordon has written eloquently, if a little polemically, on the perils of a divided sermon.[1] Near the top of the list is the fact that when confronted with such mixed messages, the preacher's hearers are unlikely to be able to discern what he actually wants them to do. The first issue, then, is that the application is divided.

---

1   T. David Gordon, *Why Johnny Can't Preach: The Media Have Shaped the Messengers* (Phillipsburg, NJ: P&R, 2012).

The thing that makes it worse is that *none* of the three applications the speaker draws out are the stated aim of the talk. His aim sentence tells us that he wants us to be more confident that the gospel is in line with the Old Testament; this is the one application that he doesn't develop. It gets a sentence or two in his conclusion, and a tip of the hat in the way the points are phrased. But that's it: there's no way that this is the talk you'd give if your main aim was really to encourage people that the gospel is consistent with the Old Testament. And that's why the application feels like an afterthought. It looks like the very last thing the speaker has done. With a talk like this you can write the outline, the introduction, the explanation of the passage, even the illustrations without any real clarity about what you're going to say in application. It comes last in the process – which is why it's not infrequent that we get versions of this talk without *any* application at Cornhill.

How did the speaker get there? It isn't very difficult to see what's happened here, although it does bring one of our sacred cows within firing range. This is a vintage State-Explain-Illustrate-Apply outline. Early on in the process, the speaker has divided the passage into three carefully crafted points, and from that moment on the points have become the basic unit of thought. He has outlined each point separately: *State* the point, *Explain* the point, *Illustrate* the point, *Apply* the point. Because application (and illustration) happens at the level of the *point* rather than the talk as a whole, the aim sentence has faded from view. He's been too busy applying his *points* to remember to drive home his aim. And because application happens at the level of the point rather than the talk as a whole, his talk is trying to drive in three distinct directions. It's not that State-Explain-Illustrate-Apply makes this inevitable. In theory, the speaker could have used his aim sentence to marshal his application even as he worked through his SEIA sets. But by putting application at the level of the point, SEIA certainly makes this sort of talk easier to write.

But however easy they are to write, and however representative they might be of our preaching, talks like this ought to bother us. Truth be told, it is not a very good talk. Let's give this made-up student the benefit of the doubt, and assume that he thought long and hard about the right aim sentence for this passage. As he was doing that, he was trying to apply the principle we outlined in chapter 1: the Word of God comes pre-applied. When we turn to the Scriptures, we don't find a series of abstract propositions, waiting for us to turn them into a way of life. We find speech-acts. We find God addressing us and summoning us to response. We find a purposeful word, that is pre-applied, that is already doing something. Presumably, this is what the preacher was trying to capture with his aim sentence. Rightly or wrongly, he thinks that the purpose of Romans is to build confidence in the gospel. And he thinks that the argument for confidence that Paul employs in chapter 4 is about the gospel's coherence with the Old Testament. He may even have spent some time thinking about how this hit home for Paul's first hearers. But then he's thrown all that thinking, that careful listening, to one side in his construction of the talk. For the sake of his exegesis, he wanted to listen carefully for God's purpose.

For the sake of his explanation, he's found a way to come up with an application of his own.

The question is this: can we find a way to write talks that avoids the perils of making application an afterthought?

Retracing our steps: the kind of application we'll want to capture

We've seen any number of things that are relevant to the way that we might approach crafting our talks. For example, we'll want to remember that we should think more in terms of the 'big beasts' of faith, hope, and love than the small fry of specific actions. Application isn't just about doing stuff. And then there are things we haven't discussed that will affect the shape of our sermons: we'll want to remember that application is a whole-church, corporate activity. It simply isn't the preacher's job to spell out the definitive application to every single church member: the sermon starts the conversation, but it's unlikely to finish it. We'll want to remember Paul's emphasis on teaching Christians to think for themselves, where we might be tempted to give them a few rules.

But the main themes of each of our three chapters suggest three bigger lessons. How might they inform the *structure* of our talks?

i. The lesson of chapter 1: Careful listening and the author's purpose

The principle we began with in chapter 1 was that the Bible comes pre-applied. We ought not to come to the Bible with an agenda, looking for a passage that will help us achieve it. We shouldn't read the Bible with a crib-sheet of likely applications, ready for the right buzzwords to crop up. We ought not to think of the Bible as a list of abstract principles, waiting for us to think up applications. The Bible is already purposeful, and it is already calling for a response. We ought to expect every part of the Bible to be summoning us to some sort of obedience. And so the task of exegesis is not just to crystallise a big idea from which we then draw implications. It is to listen carefully for the author's purpose, to hear the response to which God is already calling us.

This will have a major impact on the way we think about our sermons. In fact, it revolutionises the way that we think about application. We tend to think that application is something we tack on to exegesis. On this reckoning, the work of exposition is basically done when we have explained what a passage is saying. Because we're Christian preachers, and we're trying to encourage our congregations, we add on some thoughts about the difference that this might make to our lives. But 'exposition proper' stopped at the big idea.

This is all wrong. If a passage really is summoning us to respond, then until we have communicated that summons, we haven't even begun to describe the passage adequately. And the *whole* passage will be serving that summons. But this means that our whole sermon ought to be serving this one purpose. To put it starkly, the application is the entire purpose of our talk.

And so if we take our first chapter seriously, we'll want to find a way to make every constituent part of our sermon point in the same direction, achieving our best guess at the purpose of the passage.

ii. The lesson of chapter 2 (and 3): Careful listening and the 'them then'

In our second chapter, we saw that the best way to feel the sharpness of the Bible's exhortation is to pay careful attention to the 'them then'. Each book of the Bible was given to a particular people at a particular point in time, and as we take the time to hear what it would have meant to 'them then', we realise that the Bible really does 'get' us. In all the most important ways, the first readers aren't so different from us. And then we suggested in chapter 3 that spelling out what a passage would have meant to this 'them then' is an excellent bridge into application. As we see why the first readers needed to hear it, we begin to see what it might mean for us.

Again, this should have an impact on the way that we construct our sermons. Of course, it's not unusual for expository preachers to spend a bit of time putting the passage in context. This frequently involves saying something about the first readers. But too often this turns into something of a box-ticking exercise. We know that we ought to show our expository credentials. We know that this includes some sort of idea about the melodic line of a book, and we're eager to show that we've made a trip 'to Corinth'. But it's just extra information. It's the bit you do between your introduction and your first point to show that you were paying attention in lectures. And so long as that's the reason we're going to 'them then', it'll make our talks feel more remote from our hearers, not closer.

This is a shame. It is a wasted opportunity. The reason for bringing the 'them then' into our sermons is not to prove that we've read the commentaries or been diligent in lectures. It is an opportunity to begin to apply the purpose of the passage. Our work on hearing the message for the original readers is a significant step towards landing the application for us. If we do it well, with enough empathy, it already gets the sermon most of the way to 'us now'.

And so if we're right to think that understanding the 'them then' of our passage adds sharpness, one of the things we'll want to embed in the structure of our sermons is the application of the passage to its first hearers.

iii. The lesson of chapter 3: Careful listening and a real 'us now'
In the third chapter, we thought about careful listening and landing the 'us now' on real, three-dimensional people. The danger in rushing to think about how a passage applies to the types of people I'm preaching to is that I stereotype – and stereotypes can be alienating. The best antidote to stereotyping is to think about some real people. But we also saw that there are three likely candidates for real, three-dimensional people to apply the passage to: first, there's the 'them then' (see above). Then there's the preacher himself.[2] And then, if we want to know how the passage applies to others, we could do much worse than to ask them.

---

2   I should do this on principle.

But again, it gives us a principle: as we seek to *land* the application of our sermons, we'll want to think hard about how it lands for us. And we may want to think about how it might land on some other real, but representative, people (rendered anonymous where appropriate).

An application-centred outline?

How might these principles cash out in the way we structure our talks? How can we craft talks that are designed to achieve the author's purpose, that really are application-centred? Here is one approach to constructing an application-centred sermon:[3]

i. The body of the sermon: implementing the lesson of chapter 1

Once we understand that the Bible speaks with *purpose,* it ought to affect every aspect of our sermons. But nowhere is this more obvious than in the way that we construct the body of our talks. Rather than seeking to *divide* my exposition into three discrete points, each with its own illustration and application, I'll want the body of my sermon to be united. If I have points (and personally, I almost always have 2-3 points!) I'll want them to work together, to build an argument towards the big idea and the purpose of the passage.

There's nothing particularly fresh or original in this thought. In *Setting Hearts on Fire*, John Chapman argues that the points in our sermon ought to be the main reasons that we

---

3   I owe significant credit to the communications workshop at Oak Hill Theological College for lots of this.

think the big idea is the big idea.[4] The purpose of a theme sentence is to articulate the main thing a passage is saying – presumably so that it can be the thing we spend the whole of our talk proving. The point of an aim sentence is to articulate the purpose of the passage – presumably so that it can be the thing we spend the whole of our talk achieving.[5]

But it does affect the way that I approach constructing the argument of the body of my talk. Rather than thinking of a sermon as a collection of three modules, each one independently illustrated and applied, we should think of it as a single argument. The key is not just to find a way to *link* the three points, so that they sound united. The key is for the points (however many there are!) to be driving towards one overarching purpose, the passage's overarching purpose. And this will affect at least the 'I' and the 'A' of a State-Explain-Illustrate-Apply outline. My biggest illustration should probably illustrate my theme sentence, not one of my subpoints. My main applications should be driving home the aim of the passage, not the implications of a quasi-independent third point.

In practice, this means that my *primary* aim in the body of my talk is not to articulate my teaching points. My primary aim is to articulate and seek to achieve the purpose of the passage, using the argument (or big idea) of the passage to that end. It doesn't matter if no one

---

4   John Chapman, *Setting Hearts on Fire* (Sydney: Matthias Media, 1999).

5   There are people who think that it'd be better just to have one 'purpose statement' to unite these two. I'm inclined to agree, but that's a debate for another time.

remembers my second heading. It really matters if they don't understand the central thrust of what the passage is saying, and why it says it.

> **BODY: A united argument for the purpose of the passage**
> Point 1:
> Point 2:
> So...

ii. 'Them then': implementing the lesson of chapter 2 (and 3)

We've seen that thinking hard about the 'them then' has a double advantage. First, it helps us to see that the Bible really is sharp – it understands us, and addresses us with real encouragements and real rebukes. And then secondly, it helps us to begin to land the application. Precisely because the 'them then' were real people like us, applying the purpose of the passage to 'them then' helps us to begin to hear the message for 'us now'.

One way to do this is to lead both into and out of the main body of the sermon with the 'them then'. On the lead in, we want to try to articulate what it was about the 'them then' that meant that they needed to hear the message of the chapter. For example, if I were preaching on Malachi 1:1-5 I might describe the process of disappointment and disillusion after the exile that had led the Israelites to the conclusion that God's love makes no difference. The advantage of leading into the body of the sermon with this description is that it means that from the outset it's clear how the passage would have bitten for the people it first addressed.

On the lead out, I might then try to spell out how the purpose of this passage would have impacted its first hearers. In the case of Malachi 1:1-5, this is clearly a rebuke: God's steadfast love has already made a difference, and it certainly will make a difference. Their complaints against God are profoundly mistaken, and if they don't realise that, they're in very great danger.

This leaves the main blocks of the talk looking something like this:

> Them then – describe the state of the them then that the passage is addressing

> **BODY: A united argument for the purpose of the passage**
> Point 1:
> Point 2:
> So...

> Them then – land the implications of that purpose on them then

iii. 'Us now' and implementing the lesson of chapter 3

Finally, we want to bring it across to us now – but we want to try to focus on 'real' people rather than our cardboard cut-outs and straw men. But this affects the beginning of my sermons. Rather than starting with an illustration that sets up one of the concepts later on in the passage (the politics illustration in our Romans 4 example), I try to use the beginning of my sermons to get my hearers to see that they have similar concerns to the 'them then' in the passage. This might mean articulating those concerns as a question that we're asking, or a pattern of thinking that we share. Bryan Chappell describes this as a **Fallen Condition Focus**, the thing that we hold in common with the original readers that means that the purpose of this passage is good for us.[6] And to try to make sure that I'm not speaking to stereotypes, I spend a considerable amount of my time thinking about how *I* am like the original readers. And then I often talk to some friends about how *they* might see themselves in the original readers. As I introduce the Fallen Condition Focus in my sermon, I'll use some of the things that genuinely make *me* ask that question (whether or not I talk about myself!).

This introduction is what I then come back to at the end of the sermon: how does the purpose of the passage now address *us*? How does it answer the question that we began with? How might it change the pattern of thinking we identified at the beginning? In other words, what

---

6   Bryan Chapell, *Christ-Centered Preaching* (Grand Rapids, MI: Baker Publishing Group, 1994). 'Fallen condition' is perhaps unduly negative. In Romans, for example, I'd argue that Paul's primary purpose for writing isn't a lack in the Romans so much as a project he wants them on board with, and it's hard to describe this as an aspect of *their* fallen condition. But it's the right sort of idea.

would it look like for the purpose of the passage to be achieved in us?

> Us now – describe the fallen condition focus that makes us like the original readers

> Them then – describe the state of the them then that the passage is addressing

> **BODY: A united argument for the purpose of the passage**
> Point 1:
> Point 2:
> So...

> Them then – land the implications of that purpose on the them then

> Us now – land the implications of the purpose on us now

iv. The seven-second sermon: a twist on 'theme' and 'aim'?

In one sense, an outline like this is all about re-emphasising the Cornhill basics: summarise the big idea of the passage as a theme sentence, and make it the main point of your talk. That's what the *body* section of this outline is all about. Summarise the purpose of the passage in an aim sentence, and make it the target of everything you say. That's what the 'us now' and 'them then' bits of this outline are meant to be achieving. Having one clear point, achieving one clear purpose, is what 'theme sentence' and 'aim sentence' were always intended to be about.

In my own preaching, however, I have found it helpful to add an extra stage. Once I have my theme and my aim sentences,[7] I try to fill out the following table:[8]

Seven-Second Sermon

Question?	
Answer!	
So what...	

The **question** is the fallen condition focus, the pastoral issue that the passage is addressing, articulated as a question. For example, if I were preaching on Malachi 1:1-5 I might write something like this: 'Does belonging to God make any difference?' If I were preaching on 2 Corinthians 4:7-15, I might write: 'Why does the ministry of the gospel look so inglorious?'

The **answer** encapsulates what I want to say in the body of my sermon. It is the big idea of the passage, my theme sentence. But I find that expressing it as the answer to a question often allows me to be more concise; it helps me to avoid the temptation to write a lawyer's summary as my theme sentence. For my Malachi 1:1-5 sermon,

7   As a matter of fact, I'm more likely to write an integrated 'purpose statement', but that's another matter.

8   I was shown this by the very helpful Oak Hill preaching workshop.

my headings might be 'God's steadfast love has already made a difference' and 'God's steadfast love certainly will make a difference'. But for this box, I could abbreviate: 'God's love certainly makes a difference'.

I fill out the **so what** box with my executive summary of what this passage means for us. This will form the basis of both halves of the conclusion – the application to 'them then' and the application to 'us now'. I think that the purpose of Malachi 1:1-5 is to rebuke Israel for their cynicism, their self-righteousness and their half-heartedness. And so I might write: 'If we think serving God makes no difference, we need to repent.'

Seven-Second Sermon on Malachi 1:1-5

Question?	Does belonging to God make any difference?
Answer!	God's steadfast love certainly makes a difference
So what...	If we think serving God makes no difference, we need to repent

There is nothing particularly clever here, but the benefit of this table is that it reorganises my theme and aim sentences towards an outline – and towards the kind of outline that will put application front and centre. The **question** box forms the basis of my introduction – I'll begin with the ways in which we ask this question, and then move on to the ways in which the first readers were asking it. The **answer** box summarises the body of my talk. In my exposition, I'll want to explain what the author says to the fallen condition focus he's addressing. And then the **so what** box outlines the implications of that message (the **answer**) for people in this fallen condition (the **question**). It's not particularly clever, but it does help me to structure my sermon around the passage's central application, rather than making application an afterthought.

Question?	Does belonging to God make any difference?
Us now	• How we ask the question now...
Them then	• How Israel asked the question then
Answer!	God's steadfast love certainly makes a difference
Body	• Point 1 – God's steadfast love has already made a difference
	• Point 2 – God's steadfast love certainly will make a difference.
So what...	If we think serving God makes no difference, we need to repent
Them then	• How Israel needed to change their minds
Us now	• How we might need to change our minds

Worked example: Romans 4

How might all this change the way we approach our sermon on Romans 4?

We have already observed that the fundamentals of our hypothetical student's sermon on Romans 4 were sound. He had a decent theme sentence: 'Paul's gospel of justification by faith for all is consistent with the Old Testament.' And he had a decent, if slightly clumsy, aim sentence: 'Greater confidence that the gospel of justification by faith for all is in line with the Old Testament.' The problem with the talk was not mostly that he'd misunderstood the passage. If good application starts with really good listening, this preacher began well. Neither is his problem that he has failed to summarise the passage correctly. Rather, it was that his application was generated from his teaching points, rather than his aim sentence. In the end, all the careful work he'd done on listening to the purpose of the passage was left behind in the study. He *listened* reasonably well, but then he *said* something else.

How might he have done things differently? How might he have made what he *heard* central to what he *said*?

i. The seven-second sermon

My first step would be to try to plug his theme sentence and aim sentence into the *seven-second sermon* outline.

First of all, that would mean turning his aim sentence into the sort of **question** that the original readers might have been asking. He has understood Paul's aim to have greater confidence in the gospel, stemming from the conviction that the gospel of justification by faith is in line with the Old Testament. This implies that the pastoral 'question' Paul is addressing concerns the perceived inconsistency between the Old Testament Scriptures and the good news of the Lord Jesus. Paul's gospel looks newfangled, and strange. Justification by faith seems to be out of step with God's promises to His people. And so the question might be, 'how can the gospel of justification by faith be true when it is out of step with the Old Testament?' Or perhaps, 'doesn't the Old Testament undermine your gospel (of justification by faith)?'

Question?	Doesn't the Old Testament undermine your gospel (of justification by faith)?

Filling out the **answer** box ought to be more straightforward. In principle, this is just a case of plugging the theme sentence into the table: 'Paul's gospel of justification by faith for all is consistent with the Old Testament.' In practice, though, it's probably worth taking a little bit of time to state that more punchily. Perhaps our student might have 'Paul's gospel lines up with the Old Testament.' Or, if he wanted to capture the sense of the passage a bit more accurately, 'The Old Testament *requires* Paul's gospel.'[9]

Question? (Introduction)	Doesn't the Old Testament undermine your gospel (of justification by faith)?

---

9   There's probably a bit more to say on the precise nuances of Paul's point in Romans 4, but this will do for the sake of the illustration!

Answer! (Body)	No, the Old Testament requires Paul's gospel.

Finally, there's the **so what** box, which ought to be a positive statement of the passage's purpose. This means that it will be closely related to his aim sentence: 'greater confidence that the gospel of justification by faith is in line with the Old Testament.' But we might want to remember that Paul's overall purpose in Romans has something to do with getting on board with his mission to the nations. And so perhaps we might say, 'greater confidence that the proclamation of justification by faith is required by the Old Testament.'

Question? (Introduction)	Doesn't the Old Testament undermine your gospel (of justification by faith)?
Answer! (Body)	No, justification by faith makes sense of the Old Testament
So what... (Conclusion)	Be confident that the proclamation of justification by faith is required by the Old Testament.

ii. A reworked outline
This seven-second sermon sets the stage for a thoroughgoing reworking of the sermon as a whole – one that uses the lessons of chapters 1-3 to put the primary application back in its place:

Us now – describe the fallen condition focus that makes us like the original readers

Them then – describe the state of the them then that the passage is addressing

BODY: A united argument for the purpose of the passage
Point 1:
Point 2:
So…

Them then – land the implications of that purpose on them then

Us now – land the implications of the purpose on us now

The body

Most pressingly, the **body** of the sermon needs attention. The body of the sermon ought to be a united argument for the big idea and purpose of the passage. But it was in the body of his talk that our fictional student went wrong: his three points were applied without reference to the purpose of the passage.

This is an expository failure. If it really is true that Paul's purpose in Romans 4 is confidence, and if we really are serious about preaching what he wrote, then our purpose, and our application, ought to be confidence too. Rather than having three points with three unrelated applications, none of them very directly linked with Paul's pastoral intention, the entirety of the heart of an expository talk ought to be seeking to achieve the author's purpose.

But as well as being the most pressing problem, it's also an easy fix. There's nothing wrong with having three points, and our speaker's three points weren't bad. Personally, I might prefer a small redraft: 'The Old Testament requires justification to be free (4:1-8)', 'The Old Testament requires justification to be for all (4:9-12)', and 'The Old Testament requires justification to be by faith (4:13-25)'. But the main thing he needs to change is what he *does* with those points: the primary application of each of them should be confidence that the Old Testament really does mandate justification by faith (assuming that this is indeed the purpose of the passage!).

The them then

In chapter 2, we saw that our application will be sharper if we think hard about the 'them then'. In this chapter, I have suggested that going to the 'them then' is a good way to transition into and then out of the body of the sermon. It helps us to feel the force of our introductory question.

There are two reasons why we might think this a good idea. First, it frames the body of the sermon with the purpose of the passage. By leading into our explanation with the reason the first hearers needed this, and leading out with the implications for them, we make the purpose of the passage much more central to our exposition. But secondly, it helps us to feel the weight of pastoral questions that we might not have had to think about.

In a passage like Romans 4, this is especially helpful. Few western Christians lie awake at night wondering whether the gospel can really be true in the light of its seeming discontinuity with the Old Testament. And so the question Paul is addressing in Romans 4 feels remote. But if we take the time to explain how pressing it would be for first-century Gentile believers – well, at the very least we would be able to *empathise* with the issue: 'Doesn't the Old Testament undermine the gospel of justification by faith?'

This question must have been profoundly unsettling for them. The entire premise of a Gentile becoming a Christian in the first century was that they were being included into the people, and the story, of the God of Israel. They were turning from idols to serve the true and living God, trusting in the promised Messiah, freely offered the salvation that Israel had hoped for. There was no history of 'Christianity' stretching back over centuries and millennia, no great global religion. There was only the history of Israel, and God's promises to them. And so if Paul's message of justification by faith, for free, for all the nations really was entirely out of step with the Old Testament – well, it would be devastating. How can you preach the fulfilment of a promise when everything about the terms of the promise testifies against you? When we feel a disjunction between the Old Testament and the New, it's the Old Testament that we tend to relegate (not that we should). But if *they* felt such a disjunction, the gospel would be overthrown. Doesn't the Old Testament undermine the gospel of justification by faith? Even if we don't feel the force of the question, it really mattered for them.

In the same sort of way, I might transition out of the body of my sermon by landing the application on the 'them then'. Do you see the point? Paul wants the Romans to understand that far from undermining the gospel of justification by faith, the Old Testament requires it. It is overthrown without it. And so these Gentile Christians can be certain – they really do have everything that God promised to Abraham. More than that, anyone who believes in the Lord Jesus can have everything that God promised to Abraham. And so they can be certain that it is right to *preach* this gospel. Wherever they go with the good news of justification by faith, whether Rome, or Italy, or Spain, they will have the whole weight of the Old Testament behind them. Abraham only makes sense now that there is a gospel for the nations. Genesis was longing for the Gentile mission.

Us Now

Finally, in chapter 3 we thought about bringing the purpose for 'them then' across to 'us now' – with a special focus on how carefully we'll need to listen to do that. It's with the 'us now' that we'll want to begin and end our talk.

In the case of our example from Romans 4, that'll mean beginning with the question Paul is setting out to answer: 'Doesn't the Old Testament undermine Paul's gospel of justification by faith?' The purpose of the rest of the introduction is then to explore the importance of this question.

One way to do that might be to look for ways in which people *do* feel the weight of the question in a relatively unreconstructed way: something like this objection seems to have been behind at least one celebrity deconversion.[10] But we could also use the introduction to explore why it is that we *don't* feel the weight of the question. It isn't that we never wonder whether the New Testament and the Old Testament might be out of step with one another. We could easily multiply anecdotes of Christians thinking that the New and Old Testaments are essentially at loggerheads. Rather, it is that when Old and New seem out of step to us, *we're* happy to acquit the New and condemn the Old. For us, it's not so much that the Old Testament undermines justification by faith; rather, justification by faith undermines the status of the Old Testament. But imagine if it were the other way round. Imagine that the sheer, unmitigated authority of the Old Testament scriptures were a given for us (as it ought to be), and the New Testament was the one that had to prove itself innocent. Then we might well ask: doesn't the Old Testament undermine this gospel of justification by faith?

It's not nearly so hard to write the end of a talk like this. Even if we have never felt the weight of the objection Paul is addressing, we can certainly feel the rebar of his answer. Paul wants us to understand that far from undermining his gospel, the whole force of the Old Testament requires it.

10   https://friendlyatheist.patheos.com/2013/07/15/the-atheist-daughter-of-a-notable-christian-apologist-shares-her-story/

And this gives us even more reason to preach it: on top of the world's need for a new verdict, the joy of salvation, the honour of God amongst the nations and obedience to the great commission, there is also this: when we preach grace to the nations, we do so in the assurance that the entire Old Testament witness looked forward to this day with joy.

Summary

Overall, that leaves us with a revised outline that looks like this:

> Us now – doesn't the Old Testament undermine? Yes, and why we may not feel the force...

> Them then – if the OT undermines, the whole gospel collapses

> **BODY: The Old Testament requires justification by faith**
> Point 1: The OT requires justification to be free
> Point 2: The OT requires justification to be for all
> Point 3: The OT requires justification to be by faith
> So...

> Them then – when Paul preached to the Gentiles, the OT finally made sense

> Us now – when we preach the gospel to the nations, the whole weight of the OT is behind us

Superficially, the difference between these two sermon outlines is about communication. One approach is essentially divided, three different sermons brought under one roof. The other is a united message – one argument, with one main appeal. One is built up from the points, the other from the big idea. One is structured as a question and answer, the other isn't.

But beneath the surface, the difference is about listening. The reason I'm so eager to deliver unified sermons, with a coherent message and a single, overarching appeal is not primarily about communication. It is true that I think that sermons like this are more compelling to listen to, and easier to respond to. It's just a bit clearer what the preacher is trying to say. But primarily, it is about listening to the Bible. If the passage has an overarching thrust, a purpose that it is trying to achieve, and if my sermon is intended to be expository, my sermon should be united too.

And so the primary strength of this revised outline is that it is rooted in all the careful listening the preacher has already done. He thought he knew the theme and the aim of the passage. More or less, he did. The chief strength of this outline is that it gives his hearers a fighting chance of hearing the same things.

Conclusion to Chapter 4

Compared to the rest of this book, this chapter might feel a bit bitty. Chapters 1-3 are a sustained call to careful listening. Chapter 4 is a set of ideas on how to draft an outline. It might feel like a different sort of book.

And certainly, this chapter isn't claiming to contain all the answers. It ought to go without saying that there is no one 'right' way to put a sermon together. I remember being told about one well-known preacher who tried to change something about his approach with *every* sermon he preached. I have to confess that that sort of variety is beyond my capability. But equally, I recognise that there are many different ways to write an introduction, or to develop an argument, or to land application well. The suggestions in this chapter are not meant to be definitive. This is not 'the' way to write a sermon that takes careful listening seriously.

Nevertheless, this chapter is trying to get at something important. The argument of this book has been that good application comes from careful listening. When we apply wrongly, or superficially, it is because we have spent too little time listening to God's Word. The key to better application is not cleverness or culture: it is to sit at the feet of the Lord Jesus. And the point that this chapter is making is that all that careful listening should have an impact on what we say. There is no good listening, and listening, and listening to the Word of God right up to the point that we begin to write a talk – and then preaching a sermon that leaves the response God is calling for as a footnote or an afterthought. At some point, all that we gain from listening for ourselves, and from putting the message into its original context, and from listening hard for the purpose ought to make it into the pulpit. What we hear should shape what we say. This chapter is not the only way to do that – far from it. But it is one way to do it.

And it matters that we find a way to make sure that what we say really is what we have heard. It matters because we are listening preachers, preachers who take our cue from the Word of God. We have heard the words of eternal life. We want our hearers to hear them too.

Conclusion: Application

When we first began to talk about this book at a small meeting in Willcox House, one of the Proclamation Trust staff asked, 'Is there a PT line on application?' There are all sorts of ways in which the answer to the question is 'no'. We don't have a set process, a method, an authorised list of questions or a nifty set of diagrams to describe the process of application. Well, perhaps we have one diagram, but I'll come on to that in a minute. We don't dictate proportions: I have been given indicative percentages for the application section of my talks, but not at Cornhill. I think we'd welcome all sorts of perspectives on the best ways to help people begin to connect what we've heard in our studies with their lives. We hear all sorts of wisdom on the subject from our guest lecturers, and we appreciate it. In all sorts of ways we *don't* have a PT line on application – and it is for this reason that this little book is not intended to be anything like the final word on the subject.

But in another sense, we certainly do have a line on application. If I were feeling very bold, I might even say that the Proclamation Trust *is* a line on the correct application of Scripture. Our basic conviction is that good preaching, genuinely authorised Christian preaching, comes from attentive listening to the Word of God. And so it is also our conviction that good application, genuinely authorised application, comes from attentive listening to the Word of God. Until you have listened long enough to know what God has actually said to us, you simply should not presume to speak for Him. This is what we are all about.

And so this is what this book has been about. From one perspective, it has been a meditation on the triangle tool: 'God spoke to them then for us now'. That's the diagram! God spoke to 'them then' – and so the basic thrust of our application will be the purpose of these words for its first hearers. God spoke to 'them then', and so we'll sharpen our understanding of what that means by drawing near to them, wrestling to understand why they needed to hear this. God spoke to 'them then' for 'us now' – and so we'll draw near to them and see how this Word for them now lands on us. But lest that seem too esoteric, there is another perspective. From this perspective, this book has simply been a manifesto for good listening. The more diligently, persistently, carefully and submissively we listen to the Word of God, the more we'll have to say. Good application comes from good listening.

There is a danger that this whole approach will be deemed out of touch. This is ivory tower application. This is the revenge of the middle class, speaking into the world from the comfort of their studies, addressing the culture from a well-kept garden. It is a manifesto for withdrawal. And so it is perhaps worth spelling out that we don't think that. We believe in stuck-in Christian ministry. We believe, passionately, in the priority of personal work. We believe in small group Bible studies. We believe in the every member ministry of the Word of God, and we believe in it enough to think that anyone giving sermons on Sunday should spend significant time amongst the people they want to win. We believe in equipping people for evangelism, and we believe in pastors engaging in that task. The very last thing we want to encourage is the pernicious idea that the pastor is a specialist in delivering monologues, hiding away until the very last minute when he emerges, triumphant, to deliver his thirty-minute address and then disappear back into the smoke. Now is the age of the worldwide manifestation of the gospel. It would be very peculiar if the ministers of that gospel behaved like moles.

But we also believe that God has spoken. *God* has spoken. And so we need to make sure that whatever else we do, we listen to Him. To think that the *primary* path to sharper application is to spend more time listening to our culture or engaging with the world or working in coffee shops is just muddle-headed. The world does not need a mirror, a preacher who can reflect their vanities back to them. Our congregations do not need a counsellor, who can hear their anxieties and jot them down. They need the Word of God. This is the authoritative Word on what we are like; this is the authoritative Word on what we need. And so because God has spoken, we *must* listen. When it comes to application, there is no substitute for time with God and His Word in the study.

The trouble with the message of this book is that it is a slow burner. It takes so much time to listen carefully to the Word of God – especially if you want to listen carefully enough to sound like you have something to say. The Psalmist could write that he had more understanding than his enemies, even his teachers, even the elders of the people. But it did not come overnight: he meditated, stored up, sang and submitted to the Word of God.[1] A friend of mine has argued that it takes fifteen years to train an expository preacher. Let's assume that he's right: I can't think that those fifteen years are mostly about acquiring technique. It's just that it takes a long time to build up the sort of understanding of God's Word that makes it clear that a preacher really has something to say. And there are apparent shortcuts. An hour in James K.A. Smith or James Davison Hunter, an hour in an art-house cinema or listening to BBC 5 Live, an hour spent reading long-form journalism, or doing your pastoral visiting, or flicking through *The Week*, might make us sound like we're saying *something* worth saying much more quickly.

And each of these have their place. But they are not our mandate. The mark of the expository preacher is that we sit at Jesus' feet. And precisely because that is such a slow burner, and it's so tempting to cut the process short, precisely because we want to *Get Preaching*, we need to find something to say, the purpose of this book is to strengthen your arm: if you want to apply well, give yourself to the task of listening to God's Word. Give yourself to a lifetime of listening. Because the only

---

1   Psalm 119:97-104.

adequate preparation for speaking *for* Jesus is first to sit at His feet and listen.

> Then people went out to see what had happened, and they came to Jesus and found the man from whom the demons had gone, sitting at the feet of Jesus, clothed and in his right mind... [and] Jesus sent him away, saying, 'Return to your home, and declare how much God has done for you.' And he went away, proclaiming throughout the whole city how much Jesus had done for him (Luke 8:35, 39).

ABOUT THE PROCLAMATION TRUST

The Proclamation Trust is all about unashamedly preaching and teaching God's Word, the Bible. Our firm conviction is that when God's Word is taught, God's voice is heard, and therefore our entire work is about helping people engage in this life-transforming work.

We have three strands to our ministry:

Firstly, we run the Cornhill Training Course which is a three-year, part-time course to train people to handle and communicate God's Word rightly.

Secondly, we have a wide portfolio of conferences we run to equip, enthuse and energise senior pastors, assistant pastors, students, ministry wives, women in ministry and church members in the work God has called them to. We also run the Evangelical Ministry Assembly each summer in London which is a gathering of over a thousand church leaders from across the UK and from around the world.

Thirdly, we produce an array of resources, of which this book in your hand is one, to assist people in preaching, teaching and understanding the Bible.

For more information please go to www.proctrust.org.uk

PT RESOURCES

Get Preaching:

All-Age
Services

Nathan Burley,
Julian Milson & Nigel Styles

ISBN: 978-1-5271-0383-2

Get Preaching: All–Age Services
Nathan Burley, Julian Milson & Nigel Styles

- Biblical explanation for why all–age services are important
- Practical tips for putting together an all–age service
- Part of the Get Preaching series

The church is an all–age family, and the whole family can grow through hearing the Word of God preached. With the Bible at the centre of every service, Nathan Burley, Julian Milson and Nigel Styles give helpful foundations and suggestions for how to include everyone in the church family in the message, before going through a large number of worked examples.

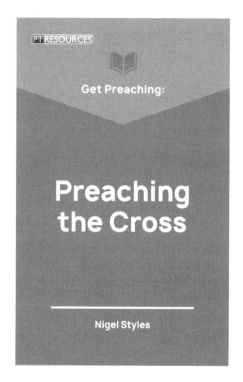

PT RESOURCES

Get Preaching:

Preaching the Cross

Nigel Styles

ISBN: 978-1-5271-0384-9

Get Preaching: Preaching the Cross
Nigel Styles

- Why it is important to preach the cross
- Helpful suggestions for putting it into practice
- Part of the *Get Preaching* series

The gospel is powerful; we just need to speak it.

In this very practical, short book from the *Get Preaching* series, Nigel Styles reminds us what preaching is, what the message of the cross is, and why that is something to be heralded to all the world. Bringing these two points together he explains the importance of always preaching the cross when preaching the Bible.

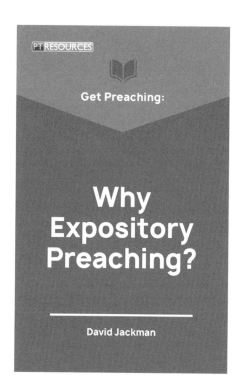

Get Preaching:

Why Expository Preaching?

David Jackman

ISBN 978-1-5271-0385-6

Get Preaching: Why Expository Preaching?
David Jackman

- Examines the importance of expository preaching
- Helpful suggestions for putting it into practise
- Part of the *Get Preaching* series

At its simplest expository preaching is preaching which allows the Biblical text to direct the contents of the message, by which the church grows and flourishes.
But why is it so important?

In this short book David Jackman explains the motivation behind this method of preaching, gives instruction for putting it into practise, and works through a couple of examples of expository sermons. This book will be a crucial tool for anyone engaged in teaching God's flock.

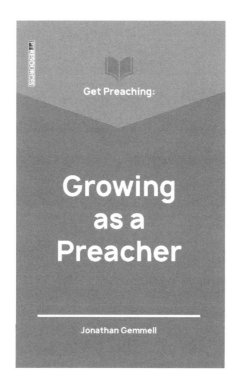

Get Preaching:

Growing
as a
Preacher

Jonathan Gemmell

ISBN 978-1-5271-0537-9

Get Preaching: Growing as a Preacher
Jonathan Gemmell

Preaching is hard work. Anyone who has preached even for a short while will comprehend the synapse straining effort it takes to write and deliver a sermon. This book is to help people progress in their preaching over the long-haul of ministry, it addresses both skills and attitudes. Every preacher can become a better preacher

Christian Focus Publications

Our mission statement —

STAYING FAITHFUL

In dependence upon God we seek to impact the world through literature faithful to His infallible Word, the Bible. Our aim is to ensure that the Lord Jesus Christ is presented as the only hope to obtain forgiveness of sin, live a useful life and look forward to heaven with Him.

Our books are published in four imprints:

CHRISTIAN FOCUS

Popular works including biographies, commentaries, basic doctrine and Christian living.

CHRISTIAN HERITAGE

Books representing some of the best material from the rich heritage of the church.

MENTOR

Books written at a level suitable for Bible College and seminary students, pastors, and other serious readers. The imprint includes commentaries, doctrinal studies, examination of current issues and church history.

CF4•K

Children's books for quality Bible teaching and for all age groups: Sunday school curriculum, puzzle and activity books; personal and family devotional titles, biographies and inspirational stories — because you are never too young to know Jesus!

Christian Focus Publications Ltd,
Geanies House, Fearn, Ross-shire,
IV20 1TW, Scotland, United Kingdom.
www.christianfocus.com
blog.christianfocus.com